Fundamentals
of
Reading Music

By Adam Brown

A combination textbook and workbook that teaches the basics
of reading standard music notation.

Cover Design: Ivan Anthony Olofernes
All music examples created by Adam Brown
Printed in the Philippines
1st Edition

ISBN 978-0-578-50611-1
United States Copyright Office number TXu001989876

TABLE OF CONTENTS

Introduction

Music is a language to its own. It takes a lot of time and practice to master any language and the language of music is no different. This book will take the readers from the very beginning to being proficient in the fundamentals of reading music.

The purpose of this book is to give the essential information in order for the reader to be able to read sheet music. The book covers how to read the note names, how to count rhythms, major and minor scales, major and minor key signatures, and additional basic musical terms.

It is not the goal of this book to be a complete text on music theory. It does not cover chord analysis and advanced theory. And by no means does this cover everything ever needed to be known in music, that book would be far too large and overwhelming. As revealed in the title, this covers the fundamentals, the basics, the most important information on how to read standard musical notation. After completing the book, the reader will be able to read music at a proficient level.

This book was written with two different kinds of readers in mind, the beginning music students with no experience as well as adults and older students who might have learned to play by ear but cannot read musical notation. Because music is the same for all instruments, this book is intended for all musicians. Sometimes a piano layout is used, but this is in no way meant for just piano students, the piano layout is just used as a visual reference for all music students.

The text can be studied independently for those wanting to learn on their own. It can be used in private lessons where students are being taught how to read music. It can also be used in the classroom when groups of students are expected to read music notation as a part of their musical education.

The format of the book is written with several lessons together, followed by a review and a written test. The lessons that are grouped together are related and will combine together to give a better understanding of the material.

Studying music is a lifetime pursuit, but this textbook and workbook combination will give the solid foundation for further study. Music is something that everyone can enjoy regardless of age. Hopefully this book can start a lifetime of musical enjoyment.

Adam Brown
Author

Lesson 1: The Staff

Music is written on a staff made up of five lines. The staff organizes music so that it is easier for musicians to read. The plural (meaning more than one) of staff is staves.

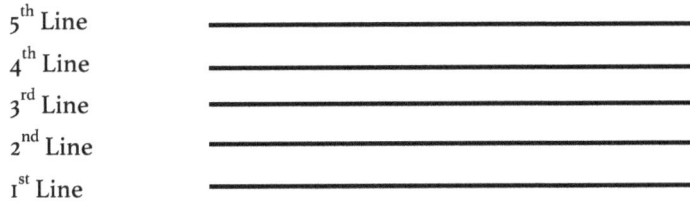

5th Line
4th Line
3rd Line
2nd Line
1st Line

Between each line is a space, for a total of four spaces inside the staff.

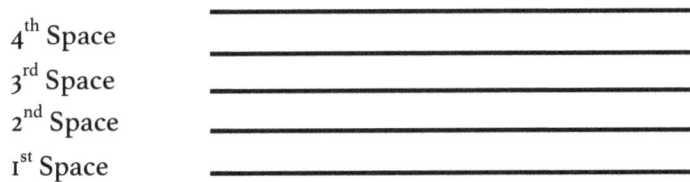

4th Space
3rd Space
2nd Space
1st Space

Music is arranged on the staff to show how high or low the note sounds when played. The higher the note is on the staff, the higher the note sounds.

The first note sounds higher than the second because it appears higher in the staff.

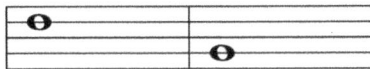

The first note sounds lower than the second because it appears lower in the staff.

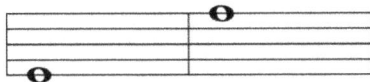

Exercises:
Draw your own 5-line musical staff below

In each example below, use an arrow to indicate the direction from the first note to the second. Write an arrow pointing up if the note goes higher, or down for lower.

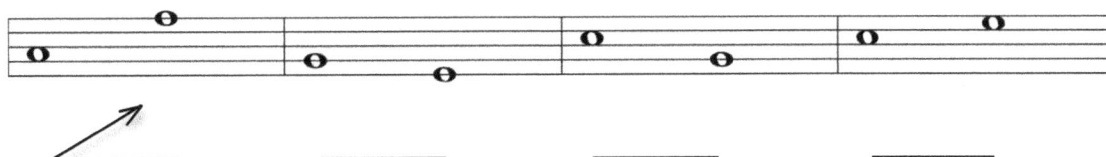

Lesson 2: Treble Clef Note Names

Music can go from very low to very high. The 5-line staff arranges musical notation so that it is easier to read a range of notes. In order to be more specific in writing music, we use the 5-line staff with a symbol called a clef. There are many clefs, but one of the most commonly used is called the Treble Clef, or G Clef. Some of the instruments that use Treble Clef include: violin, flute, saxophone, piano, and female voice.

This is what a Treble Clef looks like. It is also called a G Clef because the end of the clef loops around the G line.

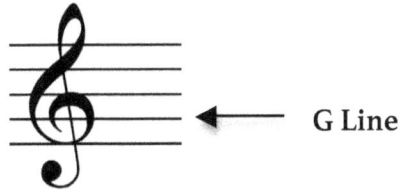

← G Line

In music, we use the first seven letters of the alphabet (A through G) to name the notes. After G, we start back at A and continue again over and over. When going one line or space higher, we go forward through the alphabet. Once at the letter G, we go back to the letter A and start over again. When going one line or space lower, we go backward through the alphabet. Once at the letter A, we go back to letter G and start over again.

This is the arrangement of notes in the Treble Clef staff:

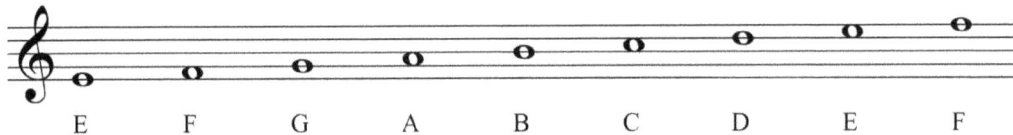

E   F   G   A   B   C   D   E   F

At first it might take time to remember the names for each line and space, but with practice it will get faster and easier. The goal is to be able to read the notes at sight, just like any language. But first, you can use some reminders to help you remember.

Lines: "Every Good Boy Does Fine" for the lines from the bottom to the top.

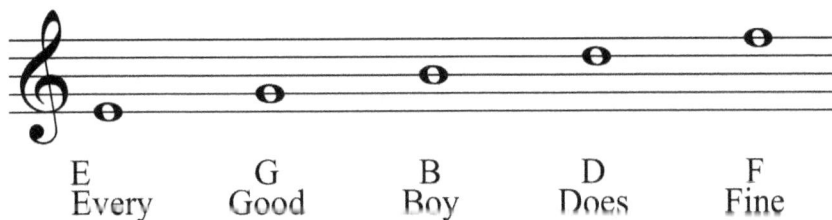

E   G   B   D   F
Every   Good   Boy   Does   Fine

Spaces: "FACE in the space" for the spaces from the bottom to the top.

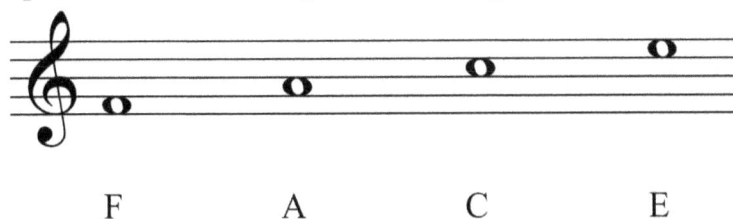

F   A   C   E

Treble Clef Exercises

The musical alphabet uses the letters _____ through _____ .

A musical staff is made up of _____ lines and _____ spaces.

Name the following notes in the Treble Clef staff:

__G__   _____   _____   _____   _____   _____   _____   _____

In the empty Treble Clef staff below, write the notes in the staff for each note name. If a letter can be written in more than one place, choose either one:

D   F   C   G   A   E   B   F

Draw a 5-line staff with the Treble Clef in the space below.

Lesson 3: Bass Clef Note Names

The Treble Clef is not the only clef used in musical notation. Another common clef is the Bass Clef, also known as the F Clef. The Bass Clef is used for a different (lower) range of notes than the Treble Clef. Some of the instruments that use the Bass Clef include: bass guitar, tuba, piano, trombone, and male voice.

This is what a Bass Clef looks like. It is also called an F Clef because the two dots of the clef go on both sides of the F line.

F Line

This is the arrangement of notes in the Bass Clef staff:

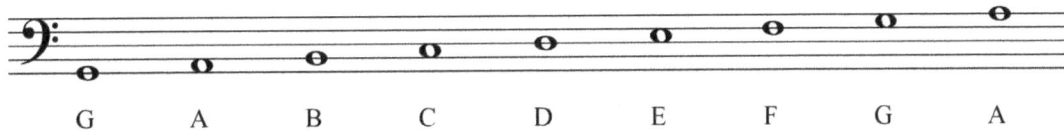

G   A   B   C   D   E   F   G   A

Just like with the Treble Clef staff, it will take time to be able to read the notes of the Bass Clef at sight. Be patient and with practice you will get faster and it will be easier. There are sayings to help remember the note names for the Bass Clef.

Lines: "**G**ood **B**oys **D**eserve **F**udge **A**lways" for the lines from the bottom to the top.

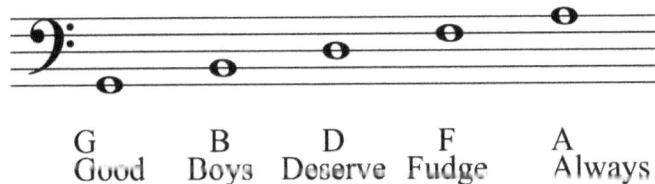

G   B   D   F   A
Good   Boys   Deserve Fudge Always

Spaces: "**A**ll **C**ows **E**at **G**rass" for the spaces from the bottom to the top.

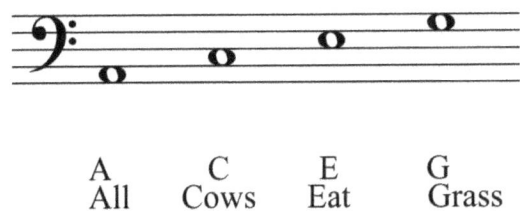

A   C   E   G
All   Cows   Eat   Grass

Bass Clef Exercises

The other name for the Bass Clef is the _____ Clef.

Name the following notes in the Bass Clef staff:

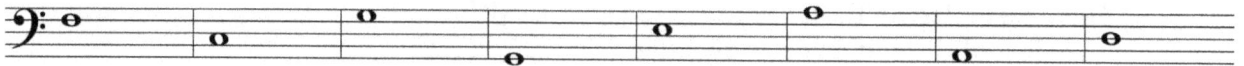

_F_   ___   ___   ___   ___   ___   ___   ___

In the empty Bass Clef staff below, write the notes in the staff for each note name. If a letter can be written in more than one place, choose either one:

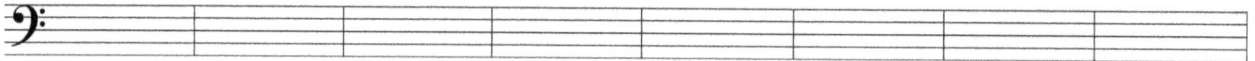

F   G   E   A   C   B   D   G

Draw a 5-line staff with the Bass Clef in the space below.

Lesson 1-3 Review

The musical staff is made up of 5 lines and 4 spaces to arrange music to make it easier for musicians to read. The higher the note is on the staff, the higher the note sounds when being played or sung.

In music, we use the first seven letters of the alphabet (A through G) to name the notes. After G, we start back at A and continue again over and over. When going one line or space higher, we go forward through the alphabet. Once at the letter G, we go back to the letter A and start over again. When going one line or space lower, we go backward through the alphabet. Once at the letter A, we go back to letter G and start over again.

The Treble Clef staff begins with the note E on the bottom line and goes up letter by letter for each next space and line. The staff ends with an F on the top line. The Treble Clef is also known as a G Clef because the end of the clef loops around the G Line.

When first starting to read notes in the Treble Clef staff, you can use the saying "Every Good Boy Does Fine" for the note letters of the lines and "FACE in the Space" the note letters of the spaces.

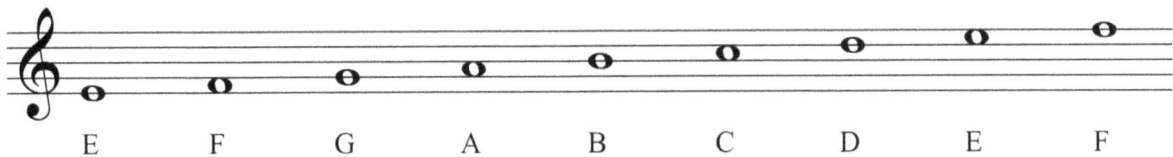

E   F   G   A   B   C   D   E   F

The Bass Clef staff begins with the note G on the bottom line and goes up letter by letter for each next space and line. The staff ends with an A on the top line. The Bass Clef is also known as an F Clef because the two dots of the clef go on both sides of the F Line.

When first starting to read notes in the Bass Clef staff, you can use the saying "Good Boys Deserve Fudge Always" for the note letters of the lines and "All Cows Eat Grass" for the note letters of the spaces.

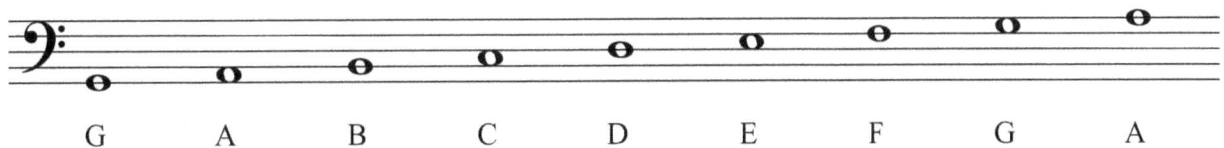

G   A   B   C   D   E   F   G   A

Lesson 1-3 Test

Write a 5-line staff with a Treble Clef in the space below.

Write a 5-line staff with a Bass Clef in the space below.

In each example below, use an arrow to indicate the direction from the first note to the second. Write an arrow pointing up if the note goes higher, or down for lower.

Name the following notes in the Treble Clef staff.

    F   ____   ____   ____   ____   ____   ____

In the empty Treble Clef staff below, write the notes in the staff for each note name. If a letter can be written in more than one place, choose either one:

A   D   B   G   F   C   E

Name the following notes in the Bass Clef staff.

    C   ____   ____   ____   ____   ____   ____   ____

In the empty Treble Clef staff below, write the notes in the staff for each note name. If a letter can be written in more than one place, choose either one:

E   G   C   F   B   D   A

Lesson 4: Whole, Half, Quarter Notes & Rests

Musical notation not only tells the musician what note to play or sing, but it also tells the musician exactly how long to play or sing each note. The five different kinds of notes we will focus on are: whole notes, half notes, quarter notes, eighth notes, and sixteenth notes. Each of the five different notes has a different length or value. In this lesson we will start with the whole note, half note, and quarter note.

To understand the note values, we need to understand the different parts of a note. Each note must have a note head and that head can either be open or filled in. Most notes have a note stem, but some do not.

Note stem ⟶ Note head ⟵

o Whole note. Whole notes have an open note head with no stem. In most music, the whole note gets four counts.

Half note, which is the same open note head as the whole note, but with a stem added. In most music a half note gets two counts, so it is held half as long as the whole note.

Quarter note, which has a filled in note head and a stem. In most music, a quarter note gets one count, so it is worth half of a half note or a quarter of a whole note.

Not only does musical notation tell a musician when to play or sing, but it tells the musician when NOT to play or sing. The time when a musician is not playing is called a rest. For each of the whole, half, and quarter notes, there are whole, half, and quarter rests. Their values are exactly the same as their corresponding note.

Whole rest. A whole rest is a small box just connected to the bottom of the 4th line of the staff. In most music, the whole rest gets 4 counts.

Half rest. A half rest is a small box connected to the top of the middle line of the staff. In most music, a half rest gets 2 counts so it is worth half the value of a whole rest.

Quarter rest. A quarter rest looks like a squiggly line. In most music, a quarter rest gets 1 count so it is worth half the value of a half rest, or ¼ the value of a whole rest.

Whole, Half, Quarter Notes & Rests
Exercises

A whole note or whole rest is usually worth _____ counts or beats.

A half note or half rest is usually worth _____ counts or beats.

A quarter note or quarter rest is usually worth _____ counts or beats.

Label the note head and the note stem on the note below.

In the space below, draw a whole note.

In the space below, draw two half notes.

In the space below, draw four quarter notes.

In the space below, draw a whole rest.

In the space below, draw two half rests.

In the space below, draw four quarter rests.

Lesson 5: Eighth, Sixteenth Notes & Rests

There are even shorter note values than the whole, half, and quarter notes and rests. In this section we will learn the eighth notes and rests and sixteenth notes and rests. Before we begin, there is one more part of the note that we have to learn. Eighth notes and sixteenth notes and rests have something that whole, half, and quarter notes and rests do not and that part is called a flag. The number of flags the note has is how we recognize each kind of note.

Eighth note, which has a filled in note head and a stem with one flag. The eighth note is held for half as long as the quarter note. In most music, an eighth note gets one half of a beat. It takes two eighth notes together to complete one beat.

Sixteenth note, which has a filled in note head and a stem with two flags. The sixteenth note is held for half as long as the eighth note. In most music a sixteenth note get one fourth of a beat. It takes four sixteenth notes together to complete one beat.

To make it easier to read and see each beat, eighth notes and sixteenth notes can be beamed together. The line, or lines, connecting the stems is called the beam. However many flags a note has, the number of beams has to be the same. For an eighth note, there is one beam. For sixteenth notes, there are two beams. In the first measure, the notes are individual and are not beamed together. In the second measure, the notes are beamed together by beat so it is easier for the musician to read.

Eighth note rest. An eighth note rest is a line with one flag. In most music, an eighth note rest gets one half of a beat. It takes two eighth note rests together to complete one beat.

Sixteenth note rest. A sixteenth note rest is a line with two flags. In most music, a sixteenth note rest gets one fourth of a beat. It takes four sixteenth note rests together to complete one beat.

Eighth, Sixteenth Notes & Rests
Exercises

An eighth note or eighth rest is usually worth _____ of a count or beat.

A sixteenth note or sixteenth rest is usually worth _____ of a count or beat.

On the notes below, label the note head, note stem, flag, and beam.

In the space below, write two separate eighth notes.

In the space below, write two eighth notes beamed together.

In the space below, write four separate sixteenth notes.

In the space below, write four sixteenth notes beamed together.

In the space below, write an eighth note rest.

In the space below, write a sixteenth note rest.

Lesson 6: Measures, Bar Lines, & Time Signatures

In music notation, songs are divided up into small, equal parts called measures. Imagine that measures are like small containers that have to be filled up completely before moving on to the next measure. If a measure is not completely filled, we cannot go on to the next measure. The measures are divided by vertical lines called bar lines. These bar lines show the beginning and end of each measure.

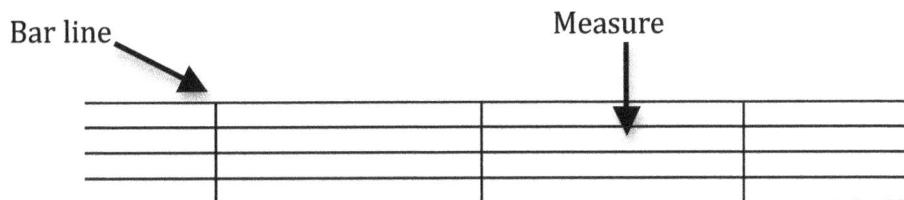

Bar line   Measure

Every song in musical notation has a time signature at the beginning of the song. The time signature gives two very important pieces of information. The top number tells the musician how many beats , or counts, are in each measure. In this book, the words count and beat mean the same thing. The bottom number tells the musician what kind of note gets one beat in the music. If the bottom number is 4, that means that the quarter note gets one beat. If the bottom number is 8, then the eighth note gets one beat.

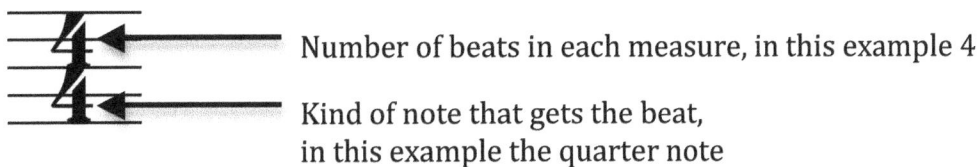

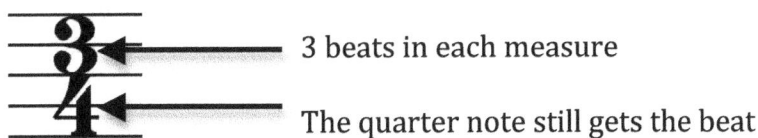

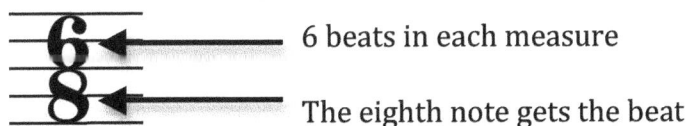

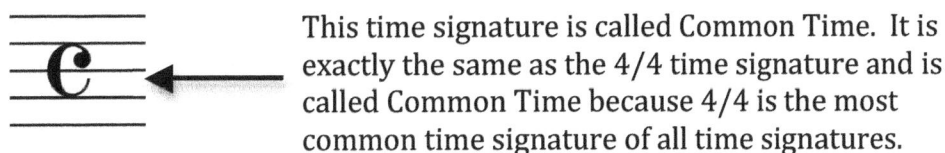

Number of beats in each measure, in this example 4

Kind of note that gets the beat,
in this example the quarter note

3 beats in each measure

The quarter note still gets the beat

6 beats in each measure

The eighth note gets the beat

This time signature is called Common Time. It is exactly the same as the 4/4 time signature and is called Common Time because 4/4 is the most common time signature of all time signatures.

Measures, Bar Lines, & Time Signature Exercises

Label the two measures and three bar lines in the example below.

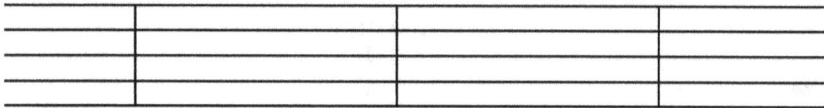

What does the top number in a time signature tell the musician?

What does the bottom number in a time signature tell the musician?

In the example below, write how many beats there are in a measure and what kind of note gets one beat.

In the example below, write how many beats there are in a measure and what kind of note gets one beat.

What is another name for the 4/4 time signature? Draw a musical staff with that time signature in the space below.

Lesson 4-6 Review

There are five basic kinds of notes and rests:

o ▬ Whole note and whole rest. In most music they get four counts.

♩ ▬ Half note and half rest. In most music they get two counts.

♩ **𝄽** Quarter note and quarter rest. In most music they get one count.

♪ **𝄾** Eighth note and eighth rest. In most music they get one half of a beat.

♬ **𝄿** Sixteenth note and sixteenth rest. In most music they get one fourth of a beat.

Parts of a note:

Flag

Note stem →

Note head →

Bar lines and measures:

Measure

Bar line →

The time signature tells the musician two important pieces of information. The top number tells how many beats are in each measure and the bottom number tells what kind of note gets one beat. If the bottom number is a 4, the quarter note gets one beat. If the bottom number is an 8, the eighth note gets one beat.

4 ← Number of beats in each measure, in this example 4

4 ← The kind of note that gets the beat, in this example the quarter note

C Common Time, another way to write the 4/4 time signature. It is called Common Time because it is the most common time signature

Lesson 4-6 Test

Draw a whole note and a whole rest below and the number of counts they usually receive.

Draw two half notes and two half rests below and the number of counts they usually receive.

Draw four quarter notes and four quarter rests below and the number of counts they usually receive.

Draw two separate eighth notes below and how many counts they usually receive.

Draw four sixteenth notes beamed together and how many counts they usually receive.

Draw an eighth rest and a sixteenth rest below.

Label the parts of the note.

Label the measures and bar lines in the example below

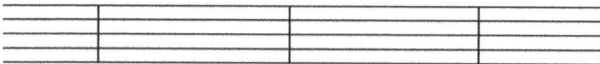

What does the top number of a time signature tell the musician?

What does the bottom number of a time signature tell the musician?

For the time signature below, how many beats are in each measure and what kind of note receives one beat?

Lesson 7: Counting Whole, Half, & Quarter Notes in 4/4

Now that we know the value of the five basic notes, we can count the rhythms in music. We will start with the most common time signature, 4/4 time, or Common Time. In 4/4 time we have exactly 4 beats in each measure and the quarter note gets the beat. The measure must be filled up completely; in 4/4 time it cannot have only 3 beats and it cannot have 5 beats.

When counting rhythms, we always start each measure with the number 1 and continue with each beat. If one note takes up more than one beat, then we connect the beats that are held together with a dash - . When counting rests, to make sure we know the beat is silent, we put the number in a parenthesis, such as (1). It is good exercise to clap the rhythms out loud while reading and tapping each beat with your foot.

The whole note and whole rest get 4 beats each and are counted 1-2-3-4. In 4/4 time a measure can only have one whole note or whole rest because it takes up all four counts. Try tapping your foot on all beats and clapping for each note on count 1.

1 – 2 – 3 – 4   (1 – 2 – 3 – 4)

The half note and half rest get two beats each and are counted 1-2. A measure can have up to 2 half notes and would be counted 1-2 3-4. Beats 1 and 2 are connected and 3 and 4 are connected. Try tapping your foot on all beats and clapping with each note on counts 1 and 3.

1 – 2   3 – 4   (1 – 2) (3 – 4)

The quarter note and quarter rest get one beat each and are counted with each beat number. A measure can have up to 4 quarter notes and would be counted 1 2 3 4. In the first measure, you would clap each time you tap your foot.

1   2   3   4   (1)   (2)   (3)   (4)

We can use this information and combine the notes and rests in different orders and still count the rhythms. Try tapping your foot for each beat and clapping only for each note. Remember not to clap on a rest!

1   2 – 3   4   1 (2) (3) 4   (1 – 2) 3 (4)   (1-2-3-4)   1-2-3-4   1 – 2 (3) 4

Counting Whole, Half, & Quarter Notes in 4/4 Exercises

Write in the counts under the notes for each example below. Be sure to write a dash – when one note or rest is held for more than one count. Also write the counts in parenthesis if it is a rest. Try clapping the rhythms while tapping your foot on each beat. Make sure not to clap on the rests!

Lesson 8: Counting Eighth & Sixteenth Notes in 4/4

So far we have learned how to count notes that get at least one count for each note. Now we will learn to count eighth notes and sixteenth notes, which get less than one count each in 4/4 time.

Each eighth note only gets half a beat, so we need to have a name for the second half of the beat. In music, we call the second half of the beat the "and." You can use the word "and" or use the symbol "&." Here is an example of one measure of eighth notes.

```
1  &  2  &  3  &  4  &
```

We can combine half, quarter, and eighth notes for new rhythms. Remember that if there is a strong beat (meaning a number) but is on a rest or held note, we put that count in a parenthesis as you see in the last two measures.

```
1    2 & 3   4     1 & 2 & 3 – 4   (1) 2  3 & 4    1 (2) & 3  4  &
```

Sometimes a note is not on the beat. When a new note is played off of the beat we call it syncopation. In the measure below, we start with an eighth note which only takes up the first half of the beat and the quarter note starts on the "and" of the first beat. That quarter note takes up the "and" of the first beat and also the second half of beat 2. That rhythm is syncopated because the quarter note and eight note are off the beat. If we hold a syncopated note through a beat, we still write the beat number even if it's not played as a new note. All beats in a measure must be counted, even if it is a rest or held from a previous beat.

```
1 & - 2 &  3    4
```

Now we move on to sixteenth notes. With eighth notes we learned to include the "and" of each beat. With sixteenth notes we need to go even further because each note only takes up half of an eighth note. We call those new notes the "e" and the "a" (pronounced "ee" as in "cheese" and the "uh" as in "lunch). Here is one measure of sixteenth notes counted out:

```
1 e & a 2 e & a 3 e & a 4 e & a
```

Many times, eighth notes and sixteenth notes are combined within one beat to create rhythms. Remember that the eighth note gets half of the beat but the sixteenth is only ¼ of the beat. Each beat much be filled up before going to the next beat. Here are different variations of eighth and sixteenth notes.

This first example, the last note is the eighth note, so it takes up the "&" and the "a"

1 e & 2 e & 3 e & 4 e &

In this example, the first note is the eighth note, so it takes up the beat and the "e"

1 & a 2 & a 3 & a 4 & a

In this example, the second note is the eighth note, so it takes up the "e" and the "&"

1 e a 2 e a 3 e a 4 e a

The following are some examples of counting including eighth and sixteenth note combinations. Try to count and clap through each line:

1e&a 2   3 & 4 &   1 &a2 & 3e&4   1e a 2e&a 3 & 4e&   1 – 2 3 &a 4

1 & 2e&a3 &a4   1e& 2 – 3 4 e&a 1e&a2e&a3   4 e a 1 2 &a3 e& 4

1 &a2 &a3 & 4   1e& 2 & 3e&a4 &   1 2 – 3 4 &   1e a2 &a3 & 4 &

1e&2e&a3 – 4 1e a2e a3 & 4   1   2   3 &a4e&a 1e& 2 &a3e&4

Eighth note rests and sixteenth note rests get the same value as eighth notes and sixteenth notes. We must count these rests, but instead of playing or singing them, we stay silent. Every note and rest must be counted. Rests are just as important as the notes!

1   2 &(3)& 4   (1) & 2 e & a 3 – 4   1e&(a)2 &   3(e)&a4   (1)e & a2 e& a(3)& 4

Music is a combination of many different rhythms and rests.   Read and count through the examples below. Try and tap your foot on every beat and cap and count the rhythms out loud. Be careful to not clap on the rests!

1 e & a 2   (3) & 4   1 &a 2 & 3(e)&a4 &   1e(&)(a)2   3 e   a 4 &   (1)& 2   3 e & 4

1   2 e & a 3 &-4 &   1 e & 2 e&(a)3 & (4)   1 &a(2) & 3   4 e & a (1)   2(&)3 (4) &

1e&   2 &a(3)&(4)   1 e   a 2 e &a   3 – 4   1   (2)   3 &a 4e &   (1) &a 2(&)3e(&)a4

1 &a(2)&   3e &(4)   1 e   a 2 &(3) & 4   1 &-2 & 3 e & 4 & a   1 e &a(2)&(3)& 4

1 e   a 2 & (3) (4) &   1(e)&a 2 e & 3 e & a (4)   (1)   2 e &(3)& (4)   (1 – 2)(3) &(4) &

1 e & 2 e&(a)3 & a 4(e)&a   1 e   a 2e(&)a (3 – 4) 1 e & a(2)(3)& 4 &   1 &a(2)(3)   4 &

Counting Eighth & Sixteenth Notes in 4/4
Exercises

Write in the counts for each exercise. Be sure to write in the counts for each note and rest as well as all strong counts. When finished, tap your foot on all beats while clapping and counting the rhythms out loud.

What is the musical term for starting a note off of the beat?

Write out the following measure in the staff based on the counts.

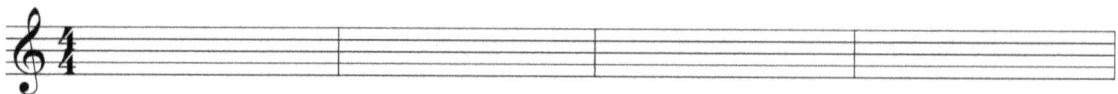

1e&a 2 & 3 4e&   1 (2) 3e& 4 &   1 – 2 3e&a 4e a   1 &a 2 & (3) & 4

Lesson 9: Counting in 6/8, 3/4, & More

There are many other time signatures other than 4/4 time. The top number, the number of beats in the measure, can be any whole number (1, 2, 3, 4, etc.). The bottom number, the kind of note that gets a beat, can be 2 (meaning half note gets the beat), 4 (quarter note gets the beat), 8 (eighth note gets the beat), 16 (sixteenth note gets the beat), 32 (32nd note gets the beat), and so on, doubling each time.

Another time signature often used is **6/8 time.**

6 beats in each measure

The eighth note gets the beat

In 6/8 time, music is still counted starting with 1 and going higher, but in 6/8 we must have 6 beats in every measure before moving to the next measure. In 6/8, the eighth note gets the beat.

1 2 3 4 5 6

In 4/4 the quarter note got the beat, so the eighth notes were called the "&" but in 6/8 the eighth note get the beat, so the sixteenth notes are called the "&." The quarter note in 6/8 gets 2 beats, so they will take up 2 numbers each when counting.

1 & 2 & 3 & 4 & 5 & 6 &

1-2 3-4 5-6

Just as before, in 6/8 time, different rhythms are combined to create music.

1 2 3 4 & 5 6   1-2 3 4 5 & 6 &   (1) 2 (3) 4-5 6   1-2-3-4 5 6

The following are more examples of counting in 6/8 time. Try and clap along while counting out loud. If an example is difficult, try and take it slower and try again.

1 2 3 4 5 & 6   1 & 2 & 3 4 5 6   1 2-3 4 (5) 6   1-2 3 4 & 5 6

1 & 2& 3& 4 5 6   1&(2)&3 4-5(6)   1 & 2 3 4 5 & 6   1 2 3 & 4 5 6

1-2 3 4 (5) 6   1 & 2 & 3 4 5 6   1 &(2)(3)4 5 6   1 2 & 3 4-5 6

Now that we know how to count rhythms in 4/4 time and 6/8 time, we can use that information to learn new time signatures easily. For example, in 3/4 time, we count it exactly the same as 4/4 but each measure only has three beats instead of four. All notes have the same note value so we can count and play easily in 3/4. The reason we count them the same and note values are the same is because the bottom number of both time signatures are the same.

1   2 & 3 &   1 & a 2   3 &   1 e & a 2 & 3   1 e & 2   3

1 &-2 & 3   1 e & a 2 & 3   1   2 & (3)   1 – 2   3 &

1 e & a 2   3 &   1 e a 2 &(3)   1 – 2   3 e & a (1)   2 e & (3) &

If we know how to count in 4/4, 3/4, and 6/8, then we already know how to count in many other time signatures. Any time signature that has a number 4 in the bottom, we count the same as 3/4 and 4/4. For any time signature that has a number 8 in the bottom, we count the same as 6/8. In the following examples, use what we already know in counting rhythms to count in new time signatures. Try and count and clap together through the examples.

12/8 Time Signature. 12 beats in a measure, 8th note gets the beat.

1 2 3 4 5 & 6 7-8 9 10 11 12   1 & 2 & 3 4 (5) 6 7 8 9 10-11 12   1 & 2 3 4 & 5 6 7 8 9 10(11)(12)

9/8 Time Signature. 9 beats in a measure, 8th note gets the beat.

1 2 3 4-5 6 7 & 8 9   1 & 2 & 3 & 4 5 6 7 8 9   1 2 & 3 4 5 6 7 8 9 &   1-2 3-4 5-6 7 8 9

6/4 Time Signature. 6 beats in a measure, quarter note gets the beat.

1   2   3 e & a 4 & (5) & 6   1   2 & -3 & 4 & a 5 e & 6 &   1 e & 2 e a 3 & (4) (5) & 6

5/4 Time Signature. 5 beats in a measure, quarter note gets the beat.

1 e & 2 & (3) & 4 e & a 5   1 (2) & (3) 4   5   1 & a 2 & 3 & a 4 e & (5)

2/4 Time Signature. 2 beats in a measure, quarter note gets the beat.

1 e & 2 &   1 & 2 e & a (1) 2 e a   1 & (2) (1) & 2 & a 1 e & a 2   1 – 2

Counting in 6/8, 3/4, & More Exercises

In the 6/8 time signature, what kind of note gets the beat?

In the 4/4 time signature, what kind of note gets the beat?

How many beats are in each measure with the 7/4 time signature?

Write in the counts for the following measures. Before starting each line, check the time signature and make sure to have enough beats in each measure, no more and no less. Once you have finished writing in the counts, try and count and clap the rhythms out loud.

Lesson 10: Dotted Notes

There are two additional pieces of musical notation that can affect rhythms. They take the rhythms that we already know and change them slightly.

The first new concept is called a dotted note. A dotted note consists of a note and a dot. The dot adds one half of the original note's value. The same is true for the rest equivalents. Take a look at the examples below:

In 4/4, 3/4 time, or any time signature where the quarter note gets the beat:

In 4/4 time, the half note would get two beats. The dot adds on half of the original value. One half of two is one. Add them together and the dotted half note gets 3 beats.
2 beats (original value) + 1 beat (half original value) = 3 beats

In 4/4 time, the quarter note would get one beat. The dot adds on half of the original value. One half of one is one half. Add them together and the dotted quarter note gets 1 and 1/2 beats.
1 beat (original value) + 1/2 beat (half original value) = 1 1/2 beats

In 4/4 time, the eighth note would get one half of a beat. The dot adds on half of the original value. One half of one half is 1/4. Add them together and the dotted eighth note gets 3/4 of a beat.
1/2 beat (original value) + 1/4 beat (half original value) = 3/4 beat

In 6/8, 12/8, or any time signature where the eighth note gets the beat:

In 6/8 time, the half note would get four beats. The dot adds on half of the original value. One half of four is two. Add them together and the dotted half note gets 6 beats.
4 beats (original value) + 2 beats (half original value) = 6 beats

In 6/8 time, the quarter note would get two beats. The dot adds on half of the original value. One half of two is one. Add them together and the dotted quarter note gets 3 beats.
2 beats (original value) + 1 beat (half original value) = 3 beats

In 6/8 time, the eighth note would get one beat. The dot adds on half of the original value. One half of one is one half. Add them together and the dotted eighth note gets 1 and 1/2 beats.
1 beat (original value) + 1/2 beat (half original value) = 1 1/2 beats

Now we will use the dotted notes with some rhythms that we already know. As usual, clap and count along with each line.

1   2   3 – 4   1 – 2 – 3 4 &   1 & a 2   3 a 4 &   1 – 2 & 3   4

1 – 2 & 3 e & a 4 &   (1 – 2) & 3   4 &   1 a 2 a 3 & (4)   (1 – 2 – 3) 4 &

1 – 2 – 3   4 e & a   1 – 2 & (3) & 4   1 & 2 a 3 & 4   1   2 – 3 & 4

1-2-3 (4-5-6) 1-2-3-4-5-6 (1-2-3-4-5-6) 1 2 3 4-5 & 6 & 1-2-3 4 5 6 1 2 3 (4-5-6)

1 2 3 4-5-6 1-2-3-4-5-6 1-2 & 3 & 4 5 6 (1-2-3) 4 5 6 1-2-3 4-5-6 1 2 3 4-5-6

1-2 3 4-5-6 (1) 2 3 4-5 & 6 & 1 2 3 4-5-6 1-2-3-4-5-6 1-2-3 4 & 5 6   1-2 & 3 & 4-5-6

Dotted Notes Exercises

How much of the original note value does a dot add to the affected note?

What is the value of a dotted half note in 4/4 time?

Write in the counts for the following dotted note exercises. Once complete, clap and count each example out loud. Be sure to check the time signature before counting!

Lesson 11: Tied Notes

Tied notes are easy to count, the ties just connect the two or more notes together, combining the note values of both of the connected notes. The rule for tied notes is that the note names must be the same and next to each other in order to be tied together. For instance, a C can be tied to another C, but a C cannot be tied to an E. If the note looks tied to another note name, it is not a tie, it is called a slur and we will learn about it later in the book.

The two notes are the same, a C tied to another C, which means it is a tie. The note value is the total value of the two notes added together.
2 beats (half note) + 2 beats (half note) = 4 beats

The two notes are the same, a C tied to another C, which means it is a tie. The note value is the total value of the two notes added together.
2 beats (half note) + 1 beat (quarter note) = 3 beats

The two notes are not the same, a C tied to an E, which means it is not a tie. The notes are then not combined because they are not tied together. This is a slur, which we will discuss later in the book.

Clap and count on the following examples below with ties. If you were playing the examples on a wind instrument, you would continue to play through both notes of the tie, but when clapping the rhythm, don't clap the second note of the tie.

1 - 2 - 3   4   1 & - 2 & a 3 - 4   1 e & a – 2   (3) 4 & - 1   2 – 3 – 4

1 – 2 & 3   1 & a 2 & 3 & - 1   2 - 3 - 1 – 2 3 &

1 2 3 4-5-6   1 2 & 3 – 4 5 6   1 & 2 & 3 4 -5 6 – 1   2 3 & 4-5-6

1 2-3-4 5 6 7 8& 9   1 & 2 –3   4-5-6-7 8 9   1 2 3(4-5-6)7 8 9 - 1   2 3 4-5-6 7-8-9

Tied Notes Exercises

Write in the counts for the following examples with ties. Once complete, clap and count each example out loud. Remember to only clap the first note of the tied notes, the second note is held out. Check the time signature before writing in the counts.

Lesson 7-11 Review

When counting all rhythms, if a note takes up more than one beat, we connect the beats by a dash - . If there is a rest on a beat, we show that it is a rest by putting the number in a parenthesis ( ).

In 4/4 time, or any time signature where the quarter note gets the beat (has a 4 as the bottom number of the time signature), we count as follows:

1-2-3-4   (1-2-3-4)   1 – 2 3 – 4   (1 – 2) (3 – 4)   1   2   3   4   (1) (2) (3) (4)

1&2&3&4&   (1& 2 & 3 & 4 &)   1e & a 2e &a 3e & a 4 e&a   (1e & a 2 e & a 3 e &a 4 e & a)

In 12/8 time, or any time signature where the eighth note gets the beat (has an 8 as the bottom number of the time signature), we count as follows:

1-2-3-4   5-6-7-8   9-10-11-12   (1-2-3-4 5-6-7-8 9-10-11-12)   1-2 3-4   5-6   7-8   9-10 11-12   (1-2) (3-4) (5-6)(7-8)(9-10)(11-12)

And in 6/8 time (counted the same as 12/8 time):

1 2 3 4 5 6   (1 2 3 4 5 6)   1 &2 &3 &4 & 5 &6 &   (1 & 2 & 3 & 4 &5 & 6 &)

The following are some examples of common sixteenth note rhythms in 4/4 time:

1 e & 2 e & 3 e& 4 e&   1 &a 2 &a 3 &a 4 &a   1e a 2e a 3e a 4e a

And in 6/8 time:

1 &2 3 4&5 6   1 2&3 4 5& 6   1 2 3&4 5 6&   1 &2 &3 4&5& 6   1 2 &3 &4 5 &6 &

When a dot is added to a note, it adds half of the original note value to the note.

In 4/4 time, or any time signature where the quarter note gets the beat (where the number 4 is the bottom number of the time signature):

Dotted half note receives three counts.
2 counts (original value) + 1 count (half of original value) = 3 counts

Dotted quarter note receives one and a half counts.
1 count (original value) + ½ count (half of original value) = 1 ½ counts

Dotted eighth note receives ¾ of a count.
½ count (original value) + ¼ count (half of original value) = ¾ count

In 6/8 time, or any time signature where the eighth note gets the beat (where the number 8 is the bottom number of the time signature):

Dotted half note receives six counts.
4 counts (original value) + 2 counts (half of original value) = 6 counts

Dotted quarter note receives three counts.
2 counts (original value) + 1 count (half of original value) = 3 counts

Dotted eighth note receives one and a half counts.
1 count (original value) + ½ count (half of original value) = 1 ½ counts

Tied notes are when two notes of the same note letter are tied together. The tie acts as an addition sign where the two notes are connected and the total value is the combination of both of the connected notes.

For example, in 4/4 time:

This would be held for a total of 4 counts.
2 counts (half note) + 2 counts (half note) = 4 counts

In 3/4 time:

This would be held for a total of 3 counts.
2 counts (half note) + 1 count (quarter note) = 3 counts

In 6/8 time:

This would be held for a total of 6 counts.
4 counts (half note) + 2 counts (quarter note) = 6 counts

Lesson 7-11 Test

Write in the counts for the following lines that include whole, half, and quarter notes/rests:

Write in the counts for the following lines that include 8th and 16th notes/rests:

Write in the counts for the following lines that include dotted rhythms:

Write in the counts for the following lines that include dotted and tied rhythms:

For each line, write in the rhythms that correspond to the counts below the staff. Some rhythms might have more than one way to write them.

1 e & a 2 – 3 4 &   1 a 2 & 3 e (4)   1 – 2 – 3   4 e a   1 & 2 e a – 3 & 4 e &

1 & – 2 & 3 e & a   1 – 2 & 3 & a   (1 – 2)   3 e a   1 e & 2 & a 3 e &

1 2 3 4 – 5 – 6   1 & – 2 & 3 (4) 5 6   1 & 2 3 4 & 5 & 6   (1 – 2 – 3) 4 – 5 & 6

1 2 3 4 & 5 6 (7-8-9)   (1) 2 3 & – 4 5 6 7 8 9   1 & – 2 3 (4-5-6) 7-8-9   1 2 & 3 4 5 6 & 7 – 8 9

Lesson 12: Ledger Lines

Earlier we learned about the note names inside the treble clef and bass clef staves. That is just one section of the notes available to musicians. Think of the staff as just a small snapshot of the notes that can be played. Music can go infinitely higher and lower than a single staff. Just like inside the staff, notes above and below the staff must be organized with more lines and spaces. We do this with extra, added lines called ledger lines, which act as an extension of the original staff and adds additional range.

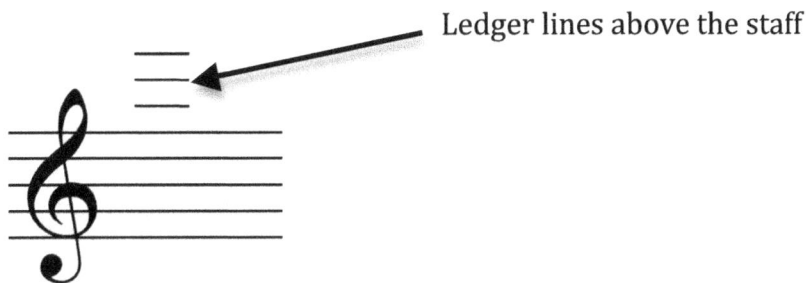

Ledger lines above the staff

Before we learned that the musical alphabet contains the letter A through G. The same is true whenever using ledger lines. When going higher and we reach the letter G, we go back to A and start over again. When going lower and we reach the letter A, we go back to G and start over again.

Below are the notes of the treble clef staff, including three ledger lines above and three ledger lines below the staff.

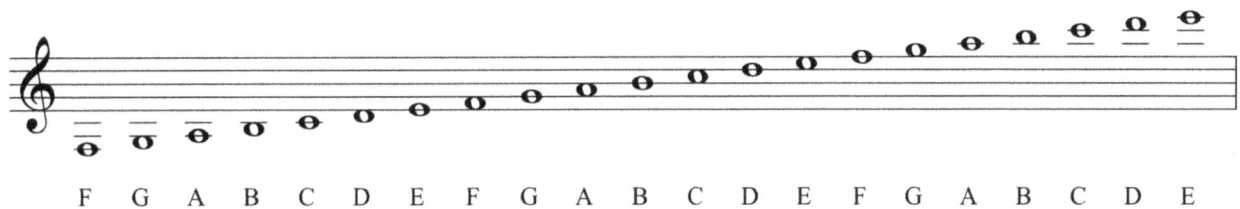

F G A B C D E F G A B C D E F G A B C D E

Below are the notes of the bass clef staff, including three leger lines above and three leger lines below the staff.

A B C D E F G A B C D E F G A B C D E F G

Ledger Lines Exercises

Leger lines can be written _____ and _____ the staff.

Draw a 5-line musical staff and two ledger lines above the staff.

Name the following notes using ledger lines with the treble clef staff:

_____ _____ _____ _____ _____ _____ _____ _____

Name the following notes using ledger lines with the bass clef staff:

_____ _____ _____ _____ _____ _____ _____ _____

For each example below, write in the note using the correct placement with ledger lines:

C above the treble clef staff

C below the treble clef staff

D above the bass clef staff

C below the bass clef staff

Lesson 13: The Grand Staff

When reading music, the treble clef staff and the bass clef staff are not just independent pieces of information. They actually go together in a simple way. When both the treble clef and bass clef staves are combined along with a bracket to the left, it is called the Grand Staff. There is one ledger line that goes between the two and that note is called "Middle C." It is called Middle C because that C is exactly in the middle of the two staves. That note is one ledger line below the treble clef staff and one ledger line above the bass clef staff.

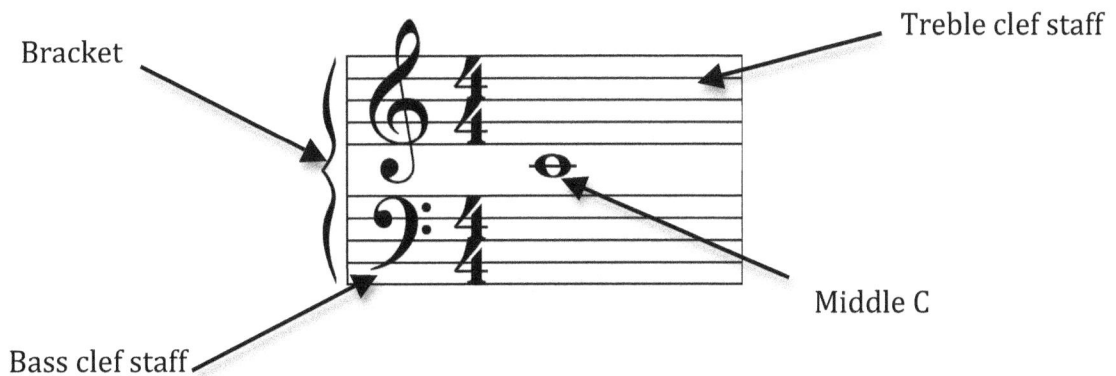

Bracket

Treble clef staff

Middle C

Bass clef staff

The Grand Staff is very common to find in music. For example, piano music is written using the Grand Staff because the full range of bass clef and treble clef are used while playing piano. Other full scores, meaning a group of different instruments, vocals, or other parts, are typically written with a Grand Staff.

Now that we understand the treble clef staff, the bass clef staff, the Grand Staff, and ledger lines, we could name any note. We could continue to add ledger lines above the treble clef staff and below the bass clef staff.

The Grand Staff Exercises

The Grand Staff consists of both the _____ clef staff and the _____ clef staff.

Name one instrument that uses the Grand Staff: _____

In the space below, write a Grand Staff complete with both staves, both clefs, and the bracket:

Name the following notes in the Grand Staff:

____   ____   ____   ____   ____   ____   ____

Write in at least four examples for each note name using the Grand Staff.

Letter G

Letter B

Lesson 14: Accidentals, Piano Layout, & Enharmonics

The musical alphabet, letters A to G, is only some of the notes available to musicians. There are notes that are found in between the note letters. But before we get to those, we need to learn some new musical notation first.

There are three new musical symbols that will help us understand the "notes in between the notes" that we already know.

Below are the three new musical symbols: a flat, a sharp, and a natural. Together they are all called "accidentals" and they affect what kind of note should be played.

♭   This is a flat sign, which looks like a small case letter B. It is written before the note on the staff. The flat sign lowers the note by one half step (we will learn more about this later).

♯   This is a sharp sign, which looks like a number sign or hashtag. It is also written before the note on the staff. The sharp sign raises the note by one half step.

♮   This is a natural sign, which looks like the number 7 and letter L combined. Just as the flat and sharp signs, it is written before the note on the staff. The natural sign cancels out any sharps and flats affecting the corresponding note.

One important thing about accidentals is that they are carried through to the rest of the notes within the same measure. In the example below, the first B has a flat sign so it becomes a B-flat. The third note is a B and because it is in the same measure and is after the flat sign, it too is a B-flat. But once we get to the bar line and go into a new measure the accidental sign no longer affects the note. In the example below, the first note of the second measure is just a regular B and not a B-flat. We call the "regular B" a B-natural because there are no sharps or flats.

This note is a B-flat because of the accidental written before it.

This note is also a B-flat because it follows the accidental sign and is in the same measure.

This note is a B-natural because it is in a new measure and there are no accidentals inside this measure.

One way to better understand the sharps, flats, and naturals is to look at the basic piano layout. When looking at the piano, the white keys are the natural notes, meaning only using the letter names. Those are the notes we first learned, the musical alphabet from A through G. The black keys are the accidentals, the notes with either a sharp or flat in their name. Notice that for each black note, we can write it using either a flat or sharp sign. This means that there is more than one way to write the note name for each of the black keys.

When going down to the next key lower, we use the flat sign. So if we start on the second white key from the right, the B, and go down to the next key, we get to a Bb, or B-flat. When going up to the next key higher, we use the sharp sign. So if we start at the far left white key, a C, then go to the next higher note, which is a black key, then it is called a C#, or C-sharp.

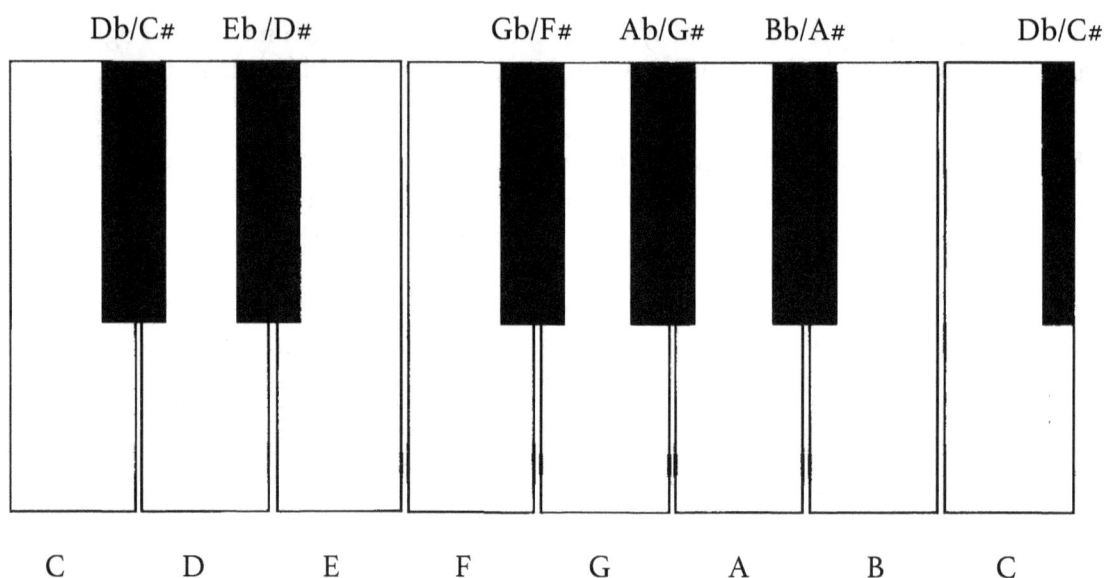

Db/C#	Eb /D#		Gb/F#	Ab/G#	Bb/A#		Db/C#

C	D	E	F	G	A	B	C

The musical reason that there can be more than one name for the same note is called enharmonics, or enharmonic spelling. By looking at the above diagram of the piano layout, the first black note to the left can be written as either a D-flat or a C-sharp. They are actually the same note, just written two different ways. That means that D-flat and C-sharp are enharmonically the same. There are also enharmonic spellings for some white notes, too. There are four special cases that are important to understand. Looking at the piano layout above will help.

- If we start at a C, the farthest white key to the right on the layout above, and go down one half step, it would be written as a Cb, or a C-flat. But as you can see on the piano layout, there are no black keys in between the C and B notes, so a Cb is actually enharmonically the same as a B, or B-natural. The same is true when going one key higher from a B. One higher should be a B#, or B-sharp, but there are no keys in between so it is enharmonically the same as a C, or C-natural.
- If we start at an F and go down to the next key, it would be written as an Fb, or F-flat. But there are no black keys in between the E and F keys. So an Fb, or F-flat, is exactly the same as an E, or E-natural. If we start at an E and go one key higher, it should be an E#, or E-sharp, but because there are no black keys in between the E and F, the E#, or E-sharp is enharmonically the same as an F, or F-natural.

Accidentals, Piano Layout, & Enharmonic Exercises

In the space below, write a flat sign, a sharp sign, and a natural sign.

What does a flat sign do to a note?

What does a sharp sign do to a note?

What does a natural sign do to a note?

Is the accidental sign written before or after the note that it affects?

What is the enharmonic spelling of an E♯, or E-sharp?

Write in the name of each note in the measures below:

___ ___ ___ ___ ___ ___ ___ ___ ___

Write in the notes on the piano layout, including both enharmonic spellings for the black keys.

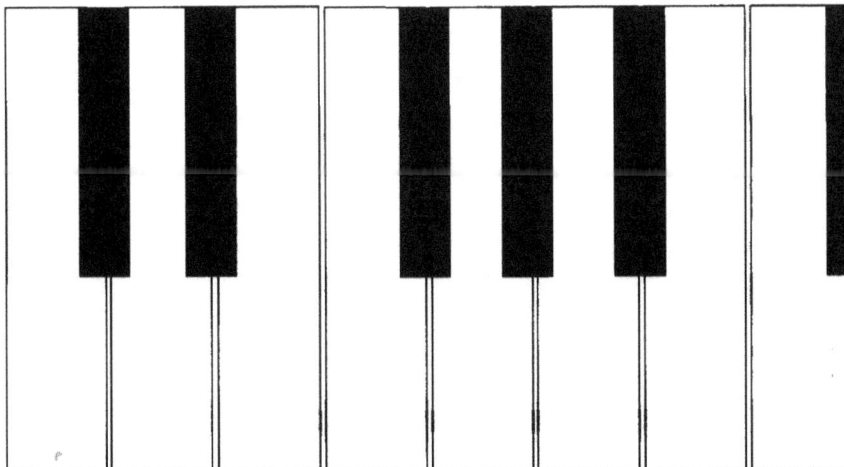

Lesson 12-14 Review

We can use lines above and below the staff to extend the staff. We continue using the sequence of lines and space to help organize the notes and make it easier to read. The added lines above and below the staff are called ledger lines.

Below is the treble clef staff with added ledger lines to extend the staff:

F G A B C D E F G A B C D E F G A B C D E

Below is the bass clef staff with added ledger lines to extend the staff:

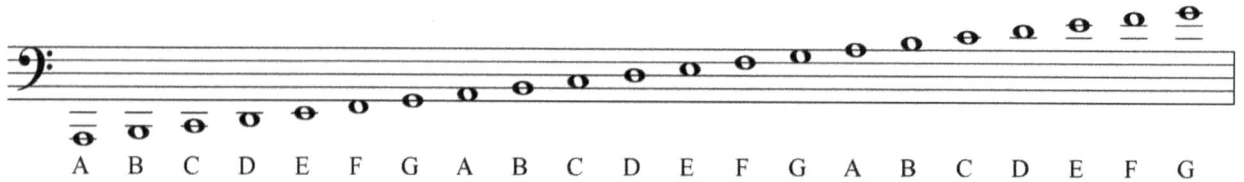

A B C D E F G A B C D E F G A B C D E F G

And the treble clef staff and bass clef staff are actually related together. Combined together they are called the Grand Staff, with one ledger liner in between the staves. The C one ledger line below the treble clef staff is the exact same note as the C one ledger line above the bass clef staff. That C exactly in between the staves is called Middle C.

Middle C. This note is located exactly in between the two staves, one ledger line below the treble clef staff and one ledger line above the bass clef staff.

We also have additional notes from just the note letters, A through G, which we have previously learned. In order to learn those new notes, we must understand new musical symbols called accidentals. There are three kinds of accidentals, the flat sign, the sharp sign, and the natural sign.

♭   This is a flat sign, which looks like a small case letter B. It is written before the note on the staff. The flat sign lowers the note by one half step (we will learn more about this later).

♯   This is a sharp sign, which looks like a number sign or hashtag. It is also written before the note on the staff. The sharp sign raises the note by one half step.

♮   This is a natural sign, which looks like the number 7 and L combined. Just as the flat and sharp signs, it is written before the note on the staff. The natural sign cancels out any sharps and flats affecting the corresponding note.

The accidentals affect every following note within the measure, not just the note it is written next to. It also affects every note of that note letter, meaning if written before an A, the accidental would affect all As, higher and lower. Once we get to a bar line and into the next measure, then the accidental no longer is in effect.

There is often more than one way to write the same note. The different ways of writing the same note is called enharmonics, or enharmonic spelling.

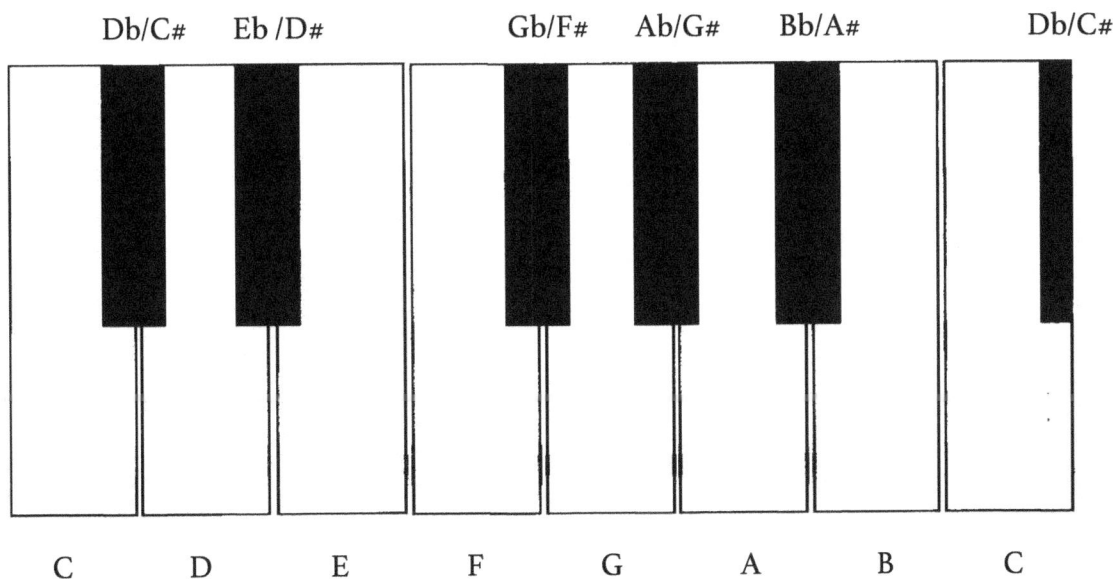

As you can see from the piano layout above, Db, or D-flat, is enharmonically the same as C#, or C-sharp. The same is true with Bb, or B-flat, and A#, or A-sharp.

Lesson 12-14 Test

What are the names of the lines added above and below the staff to extend the range?

What is the name of the large staff that consists of both the treble clef and bass clef staves?

What is the name of the note located exactly between the treble and bass clef staves?

Name the following notes:

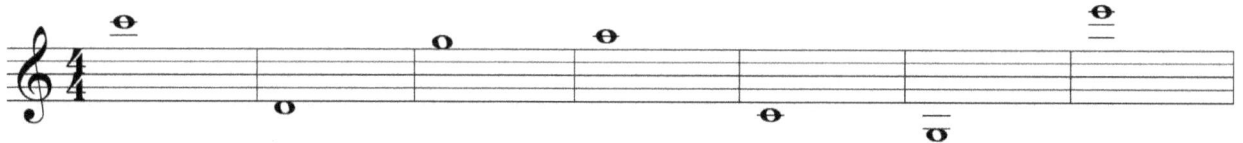

___   ___   ___   ___   ___   ___   ___

Name the following notes:

___   ___   ___   ___   ___   ___

Name the following notes:

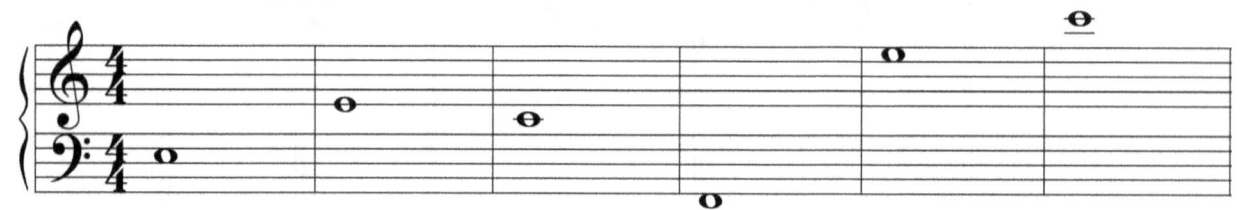

___   ___   ___   ___   ___   ___

To the right of each accidental, write the name of the symbol and what it does to the note:

♭

♯

♮

Write in the names of the notes below, including the accidentals. Remember that accidentals carry through to the end of the measure and no longer affect notes beyond the bar line.

___   ___   ___   ___   ___   ___   ___   ___   ___   ___   ___   ___

Label the names for each key on the piano. For the black keys at the top, write in both possible names for each key.

We learned earlier that E#, or E-sharp, is the same as F, or F-natural and Bb, or B-flat, is the same as A#, or A-sharp. What is the musical term for two names for the exact same note?

Lesson 15: Half Steps, Whole Steps, & Octaves

We have now learned all of the note names and the accidentals. In this next lesson we will learn about half steps and whole steps. Going back to the piano layout example, a half step is the distance between two keys that are exactly next to each other. A whole step is the distance of two keys with one key in between; this is also double the distance of a half step. A whole step is the same as two half steps. Look at the piano layout below to see half steps and whole steps:

The distance from C to C# is a half step as the two keys are directly next to each other.

The distance from F# to G# (or Gb to Ab) is a whole step because there is one additional key in between them.

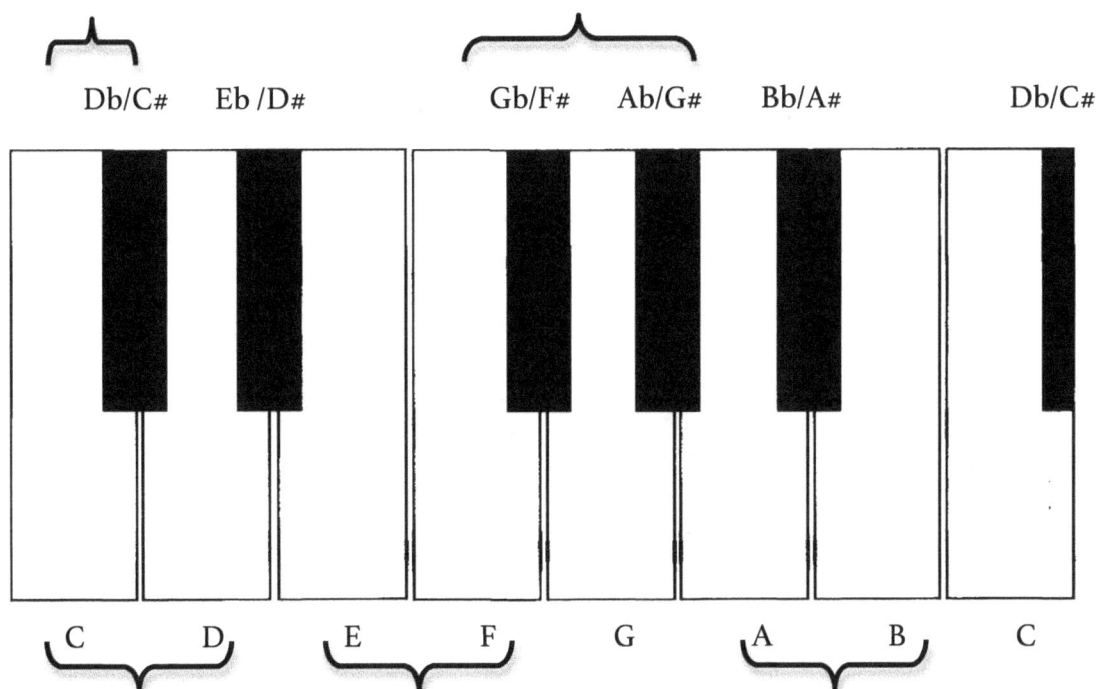

Db/C# Eb /D#   Gb/F# Ab/G# Bb/A#   Db/C#

C   D   E   F   G   A   B   C

The distance from C to D is a whole step as there is one additional key in between them.

The distance from E to F is a half step as the two keys are directly next to each other.

The distance from A to B is a whole step as there is one additional key in between them.

The distance between two different notes is called an interval.

The distance from one note letter back to the same note letter is called an Octave (i.e. A to A). The prefix "oct-" refers to the number eight, just the same as an octagon has eight sides. It is called an octave because it contains eights notes (A-B-C-D-E-F-G-A). The distance, or interval, from A to the next highest A is one octave. The octave can be above or below. Take the piano layout above and the first white key, the lowest C, is one octave lower than the last white key, the highest C. Below is one octave in musical notation.

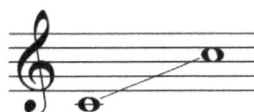

Half Steps, Whole Steps, & Octaves
Exercises

A _____ step is the distance, or interval, between two keys on the piano directly next to each other.

A _____ step is the distance, or interval, between two keys on the piano that have one additional key in between them.

A whole steps consists of how many half steps?
a) one   b) two   c) three   d) four

Write in the distance, or interval, for each other notes below. Use the included piano layout to visualize the notes.

Db/C#   Eb /D#   Gb/F#   Ab/G#   Bb/A#   Db/C#

C   D   E   F   G   A   B   C

_____   _____   _____   _____

What is the distance, or interval, called from one note letter to the same note letter above or below (i.e. A to A, or C to C)?

Lesson 16: Major, Minor, & Chromatic Scales

One common element is music is the use of scales. There are many, many kinds of scales but for this book we will focus on just three kinds: major, minor, and chromatic. When going up the scale it is called ascending and when going down the scale it is called descending.

Scales can start on any note and is just a combination of different intervals. Each of the scales use one octave of notes, but the notes in between that are used are different from major to minor to chromatic scales. The name of the scale comes from the starting note. For example, a C Major scale starts on the note C and goes through one octave to the next C above.

For major scales we will use from C to C because when using just the white keys of the piano, or just the natural notes using only the letters, is actually a major scale. The whole steps are on the bottom and half steps on the top.

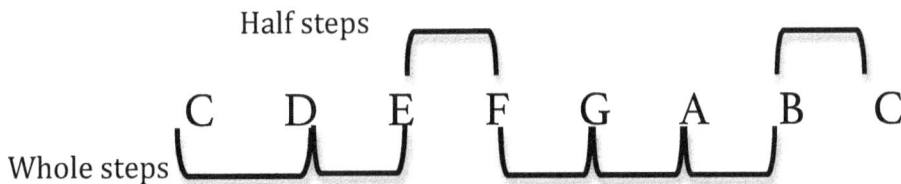

The sequence for all major scales is whole step, whole step, half step, whole step, whole step, whole step, half step. This is true for every major scale.

For minor scales we will use A to A because when using just the white keys of the piano, or just the natural notes using only the letter, is actually a minor scale. The whole steps are on the bottom and half steps on top.

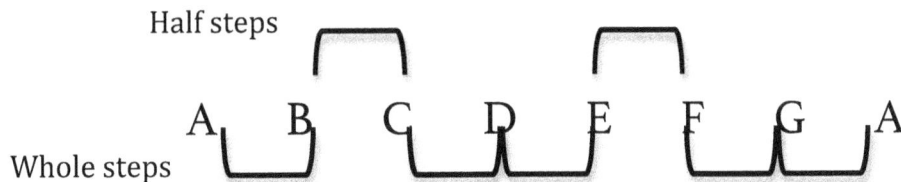

The sequence for all minor scales is whole step, half step, whole step, whole step, half step, whole step, whole step. This is true for every minor scale.

Chromatic scales are easier to remember, because they use every one of the twelve half steps in the octave of notes. The distance between each note is one half step. Below is the C chromatic scale using sharps:

C   C#   D   D#   E   F   F#   G   G#   A   A#   B   C

Each major scale follows the exact same pattern of whole and half steps. In both major and minor scales, the next note always follows in alphabetical order. Below are the major scales, plus the enharmonic equivalents for some sharp and flat keys. See if you can follow the pattern of whole and half steps in each scale. Remember on the descending side, the accidentals carry through.

C Major (no flats or sharps)

C D E F G A B C B A G F E D C

C# Major (7 sharps- C#, D#, E#, F#, G#, A#, B#)

C# D# E# F# G# A# B# C# B# A# G# F# E# D# C#

Db Major (enharmonically the same as C#)(5 flats- Db, Eb, Gb, Ab, Bb)

Db Eb F Gb Ab Bb C Db C Bb Ab Gb F Eb Db

D major (2 sharps- F#, C#)

D E F# G A B C# D C# B A G F# E D

Eb Major (3 flats- Eb, Ab, Bb)

Eb F G Ab Bb C D Eb D C Bb Ab G F Eb

E Major (4 sharps- F#, G#, C#, D#)

E F# G# A B C# D# E D# C# B A G# F# E

F Major (1 flat- Bb)

F G A Bb C D E F E D C Bb A G F

F# Major (7 sharps- F#, G#, A#, C#, D#, E#, F#)

F# G# A# B C# D# E# F# E# D# C# B A# G# F#

G Major (1 sharp- F#)

G A B C D E F# G F# E D C B A G

Ab Major (4 flats- Ab, Bb, Db, Eb)

Ab Bb C Db Eb F G Ab G F Eb Db C Bb Ab

A Major (3 sharps- C#, F#, G#)

A B C# D E F# G# A G# F# E D C# B A

Bb Major (2 flats- Bb, Eb)

Bb C D Eb F G A Bb A G F Eb D C Bb

B Major (5 sharps- C#, D#, F#, G#, A#)

B C# D# E F# G# A# B A# G# F# E D# C# B

Each minor scale also follows the same pattern of whole and half steps. Just as with the major scales, each note of the scale follows through the musical alphabet. As with the major scales, see if you can follow the pattern of whole and half steps in each scale. Remember that the accidentals carry through to the descending side of the scale.

A minor (no sharps of flats)

A B C D E F G A G F E D C B A

Bb minor (5 flats- Bb, Db, Eb, Gb, Ab)

Bb C Db Eb F Gb Ab Bb Ab Gb F Eb Db C Bb

B minor (2 sharps- C#, F#)

B C# D E F# G A B A G F# E D C# B

C minor (3 flats- Eb, Ab, Bb)

C D Eb F G Ab Bb C Bb Ab G F Eb D C

C# minor (4 sharps- C#, D#, F#, G#)

C# D# E F# G# A B C# B A G# F# E D# C#

D minor (1 flat- Bb)

D E F G A Bb C D C Bb A G F E D

D# minor (6 sharps- D#, E#, F#, G#, A#, C#)

D# E# F# G# A# B C# D# C# B A# G# F# E# D#

E minor (1 sharp- F#)

E F# G A B C D E D C B A G F# E

F minor (4 flats- Ab, Bb, Db, Eb)

F G Ab Bb C Db Eb F Eb Db C Bb Ab G F

F# minor (3 sharps- F#, G#, C#)

F# G# A B C# D E F# E D C# B A G# F#

G minor (2 flats- Bb, Eb)

G A Bb C D Eb F G F Eb D C Bb A G

G# minor (5 sharps- G#, A#, C#, D#, F#)

G# A# B C# D# E F# G# F# E D# C# B A# G#

Ab minor (7 flats- Ab, Bb, Cb, Db, Eb, Fb, Gb)

Ab Bb Cb Db Eb Fb Gb Ab Gb Fb Eb Db Cb Bb Ab

Major, Minor, & Chromatic Scale Exercises

Write out the sequence of whole and half steps for a major scale.

Write out the sequence of whole and half steps for a minor scale.

Write out the complete C chromatic scale from C to C.

Going up the scale is called _____. Going down the scale is called _____.

Write in the correct accidentals for each of the following scales:

D Major

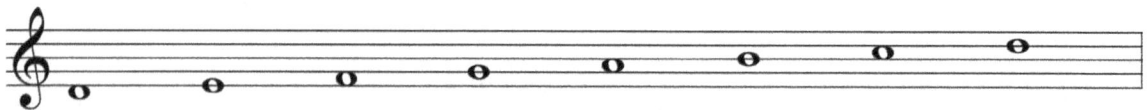

Bb Major

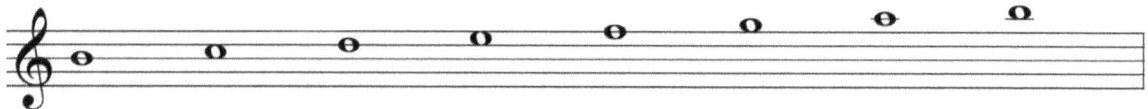

Ab Major

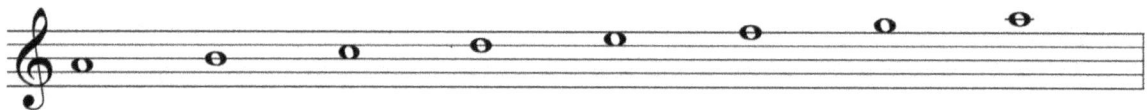

F minor

C minor

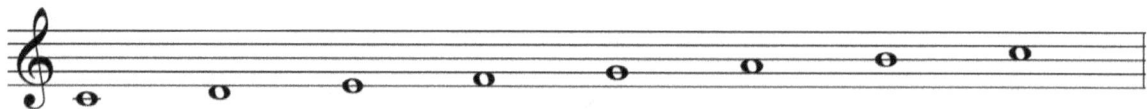

Lesson 15-16 Review

Music is made up of different intervals, or distance between notes. All intervals can be broken down into combinations of whole and half steps. To better see whole and half steps, below is the layout of a piano. Half steps are the keys directly next to each other. For example, when going from E to F, they are directly next to each other without a key in between so they are one half step apart. Whole steps are notes that have one note in between them. For example, C and D have one key in between them, the Db/C# key, so C and D are one whole step apart.

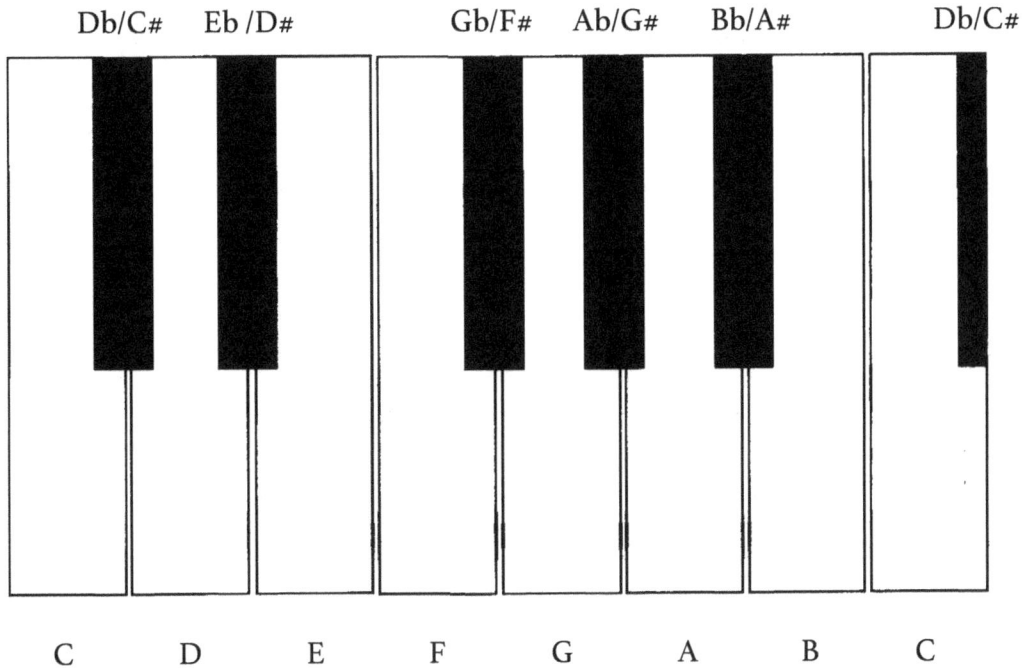

Db/C#	Eb /D#		Gb/F#	Ab/G#	Bb/A#		Db/C#

C	D	E	F	G	A	B	C

Another important interval in music is called the octave. An octave is a group of 8 notes, as the prefix "oct-" means the number 8. In music, an octave is the distance going higher or lower from one note letter until we get back to the same note letter (i.e. from C to C). Below is an example of one octave:

From C to C is one octave

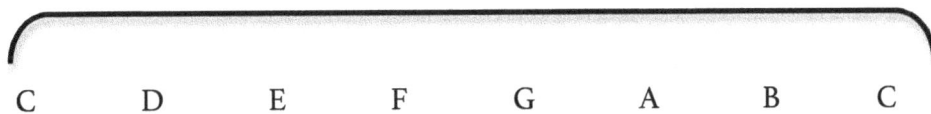

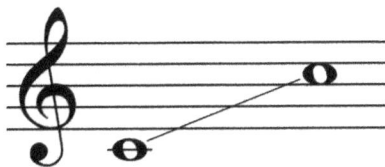

C   D   E   F   G   A   B   C

One octave, C to C, in musical notation

Three basic scales in music are: major, minor, and chromatic. Each scale is made up of different intervals between the notes. For major and minor scales, the scale is named for the starting note and the intervals used in between. For example, a C Major scale starts on the note C and goes up one octave until we get to the next C. In both major and minor scales, the note letters are used alphabetically in order (i.e. C-D-E-F-G-A-B-C). While most scales use accidentals, all major and minor scales still use the note letters in the octave in order.

In all major scales, this is the sequence of whole and half steps:

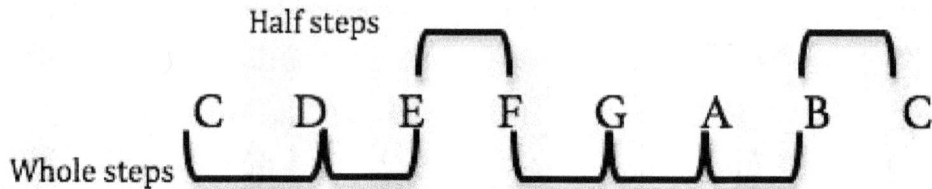

In musical notation, the C Major scale:

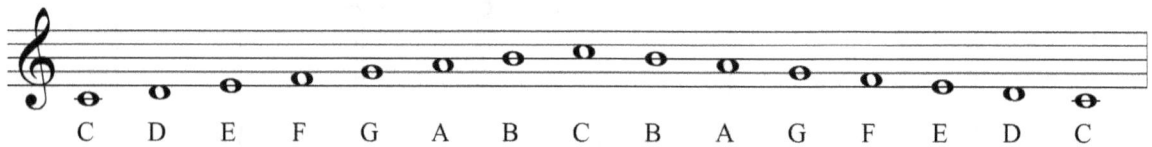

C D E F G A B C B A G F E D C

In all minor scales, this is the sequence of whole and half steps:

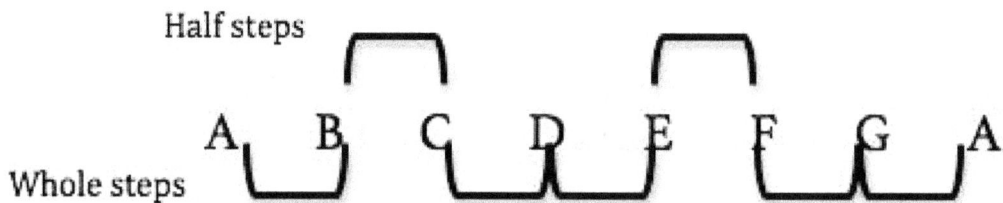

In musical notation, the A minor scale:

A B C D E F G A G F E D C B A

The chromatic scale is one octave of notes going up by a half step each time. Chromatic scales include all 12 notes in between notes of the same letter:

C C# D D# E F F# G G# A A# B C

Lesson 15-16 Test

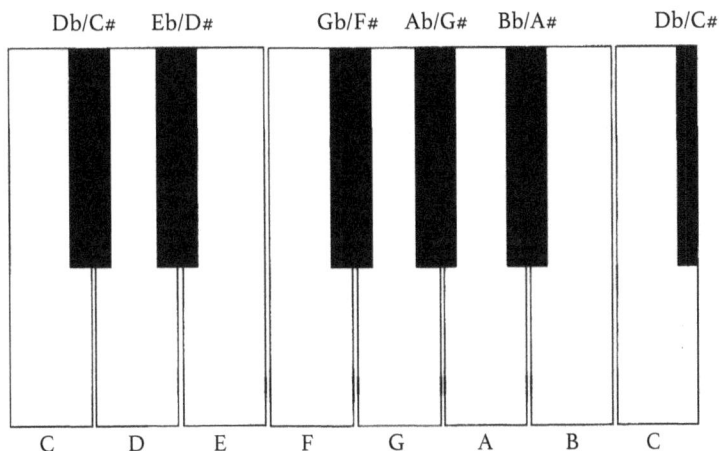

Using the piano layout above, write in the following intervals:

_____ step

_____ step

_____ step

_____ step

How many note letters are in the interval of an octave?
a) four   b) five   c) eight   d) six

Write out the sequence of intervals for a major scale using whole and half steps:

Write out the sequence of intervals for a minor scale: using whole and half steps:

Write in the correct accidentals for the following scales:

D Major scale

C minor scale

Lesson 17: Major Key Signatures

In previous lessons we learned about accidentals and when writing the scales, we wrote them in before each note when needed. There is a quicker way, whenever the same accidentals are needed throughout a piece of music. Each piece of music is written in a particular key and at the beginning of the piece of music there is something called a key signature. If an accidental is found in the key signature, then it will affect all notes in the music for that note name, including all octaves, unless a natural sign cancels it out. The key signatures are directly related to the scales that we have just learned in the previous lessons. There are major keys and minor keys. Whichever notes are sharp or flat in the particular scale are exactly the same in the corresponding key signature.

In this lesson we will focus on the major key signatures. First, we will learn the major key signatures that use the flat symbols. The flat symbols always go in a specific order in the key signature. The order of the flats in the key signature is Bb, Eb, Ab, Db, Gb, Cb, Fb.

The following are the major key signatures with flats. We will start with zero flats and then add one each time as we go along.

C Major (zero flats)

F Major (1 flat)

Bb Major (2 flats)

Eb Major (3 flats)

Ab Major (4 flats)

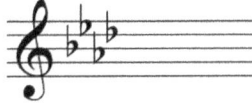

Db Major (5 flats)

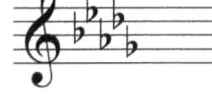

Gb Major (6 flats)

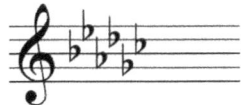

Cb Major (7 flats)

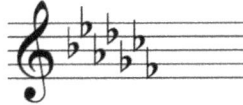

At first it will take memorizing each key signature, but over time the goal is to be able to know the key signatures by sight. There is a trick to tell the name of the key signature if we know it is major and it uses flats. For C and F we just have to memorize them, but starting at Bb, the second to the last flat is the name of the major key signature.

Bb is second to last flat, the key is Bb Major

Db is the second to last flat, the key is Db Major

Now we will move on to major key signatures that use sharps. Just as there is a specific order for the flats, there is a specific order for sharps as well. The sharps must be added in the order of: F#, C#, G#, D#, A#, E#, B#. If you look closely you will notice that they are in the opposite order of the flats.

C Major (zero sharps)

G Major (1 sharp)

D Major (2 sharps)

A Major (3 sharps)

E Major (4 sharps)

B Major (5 sharps)

F# Major (6 sharps)

C# Major (7 sharps)

Just as there was a trick to figuring out flat key signatures, there is a trick for major key signatures with sharps. Find the last sharp in the key signature and the key is one half step higher than that sharp. Remember that sharps will carry through, so if that note already has a sharp sign, then the key is sharp as well.

The last sharp is C sharp. Up one half step is D, the key is D Major.

The last key sharp is E sharp. Up one half step is F sharp (remember the F is sharp from the key signature). The key is F sharp Major.

Major Key Signature Exercises

What is the order of the flats added for major key signatures?

What is the order of the sharps added for major key signatures?

How many flats are in the key signature for Eb Major?

How many sharps are in the key signature for G Major?

Write the name for each major key signature.

   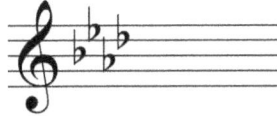

_____ Major   _____ Major

Write in the correct accidentals for each major key signature.

A Major   Bb Major

Db Major   D Major

F# Major   F Major

Lesson 18: Minor Key Signatures

Just as there were both major and minor scales, there are also major and minor key signatures. In the previous lesson we learned all of the major keys signatures, with both sharps and flats, and how they related to the major scales. The same is true with the minor key signatures.

Flats and sharps are added to the key signatures in exactly the same order as they were added with the major key signatures. If you look closely you might also notice that the same key signatures are used in minor keys that were used in major keys. The major and minor keys that use the same key signature are called "relative" to each other, meaning that they are related. For instance, the key of C Major uses no sharps or flats. The same is true of the key of A minor. That means that A minor is the relative minor key of C Major, and C Major is the relative major key of A minor. Because neither uses any sharps or flats, their key signatures are exactly the same. If we look at the corresponding major scale, the name of the relative minor key is the 6th note of the major scale. Using C Major as the example again, the 6th note of the C Major scale is A. The relative minor key of C Major is A minor. In Bb Major, the 6th note of the major scale is G and G is the relative minor key.

The 6th note of the Bb Major scale is G. G minor is the relative minor key of C Major.

Bb   C   D   Eb   F   G   A   Bb   A   G   F   Eb   D   C   Bb

The following are the key signatures for minor keys using flats. They are shown in order of increasing number of flats. For reference, their relative major key signature is also listed.

A minor (zero flats)
(Relative Major: C Major)

D minor (1 flat)
(Relative Major: F Major)

G minor (2 flats)
(Relative Major: Bb Major)

C minor (3 flats)
(Relative Major: Eb Major)

F minor (4 flats)
(Relative Major: Ab Major)

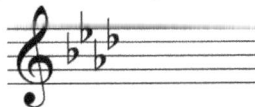

Bb minor (5 flats)
(Relative Major: Db Major)

Eb minor (6 flats)
(Relative Major: Gb Major)

Ab minor (7 flats)
(Relative Major: Cb Major)

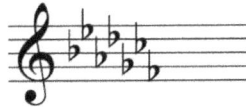

Next we move on to the minor key signatures that use sharps. The sharps are added in the same order as they were in the major key signatures. The minor key signatures with flats have relative major key signatures, meaning their key signatures are the same, and minor key signatures with sharps also have relative major key signatures.

The following are the key signatures for minor keys using sharps. They are shown in order of increasing number of sharps. For reference, their relative major key signature is also listed.

A minor (zero sharps)
(Relative Major: C Major)

E minor (1 sharp)
(Relative Major: G Major)

B minor (2 sharps)
(Relative Major: D Major)

F# minor (3 sharps)
(Relative Major: A Major)

C# minor (4 sharps)
(Relative Major: E Major)

G# minor (5 sharps)
(Relative Major: B Major)

D# minor (6 sharps)
(Relative Major: F# Major)

A# minor (7 sharps)
(Relative Major: C# Major)

We can use the same system to determine the relative majors and minors as we did with the flats. Take the major key and the relative minor is the minor key signature of the 6th note of the scale. We will use E Major in the example below:

The 6th note of the E Major scale is C#. C# minor is the relative minor of E Major.

E F# G# A B C# D# E D# C# B A G# F# E

Minor Key Signature Exercises

The relative minor is the _____ note of the corresponding major scale.

a) third   b) fourth   c) sixth   d) seventh

How many flats are in the key signature of C minor?

How many sharps are in the key signature of B minor?

Write the name for each minor key signature.

_____ minor   _____ minor

Write in the correct accidentals for each key signature.

G minor   Bb minor

F# minor   D minor

E minor   Eb minor

Lesson 17-18 Review

Major key signatures are directly related to their major scale equivalents. The same notes that are sharp or flat in a major scale are present in the major key signature.

The flats are added to the major key signature in the following order:
Bb, Eb, Ab, Db, Gb, Cb, Fb

The sharps are added to the major key signature in the following order:
F#, C#, G#, D#, A#, E#, B# (notice is it the opposite order as the flats)

A quick way to check the major key signature with flats is that the second to last flat is the name of the major key signature:

The second to last flat in the key signature is Ab. This is the key signature for Ab Major.

A quick way to check the major key signature with sharps is the name of the major key signature is one half step up from the last sharp in the key signature:

The last sharp in the key signature is C#. One half step up from C# is D. This is the key signature for D Major.

There are also key signatures for minor keys. Sharps and flats are added to the key signature in the same order. There is a relative minor key signature for every major key signature, which means they have the same key signature. To determine the relative minor key, take the major scale and the relative minor is the 6th note of the major scale.

In the Eb Major scale, the note C is the 6th note of the scale. C is the relative minor of Eb Major.

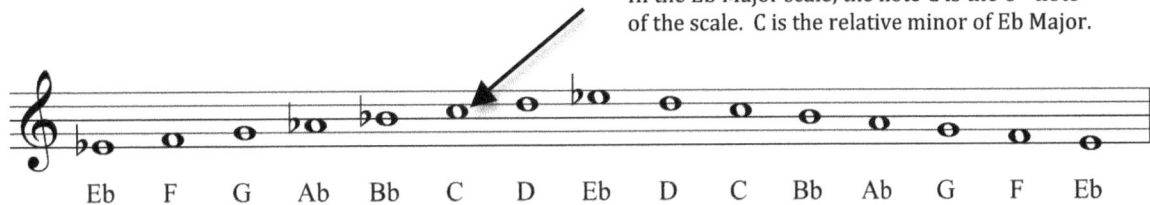

| Eb | F | G | Ab | Bb | C | D | Eb | D | C | Bb | Ab | G | F | Eb |

Refer to the full lessons to for all of the Major and minor key signatures.

Lesson 17-18 Test

Write out the order of flats for major key signatures.

Write out the order of sharps for the major key signatures.

The relative minor is found on the _____ note of the corresponding major scale.

a) third   b) sixth   c) fifth   d) fourth

Write in the name for each major key signature.

_____ Major   _____ Major   _____ Major

Write in the name for each minor key signature.

_____ minor   _____ minor   _____ minor

Write in the correct accidentals for the following major keys:
   F Major   G Major   Eb Major

Write in the correct accidentals for the following minor keys:
   D minor   G minor   F minor

Lesson 19: Dynamic Markings

There is another aspect of music that is very important and that is how loud or soft the music is supposed to be played. Dynamics is the musical term for how loud or soft to play the music. There are a variety of musical terms that are used to indicate the correct dynamic level. Most of the dynamic terms come from the Italian language. It is important to note that dynamics are a type of relative term, meaning they are not exact, but they are just a way to relate loud and soft together. The following are the most commonly used dynamic terms:

pp   Pianissimo- very soft

p   Piano- soft

mp   Mezzo piano- moderately soft

mf   Mezzo forte- moderately loud

f   Forte- loud

ff   Fortissimo- very loud

There are also some musical terms that tell the musician to change dynamics.

cresc   Crescendo, meaning to get louder

decresc   Decrescendo, meaning to get softer

fp   Fortepiano, play the first note loudly and immediately get soft

sfz   Sforzando, play the note very loud

Dynamic Markings Exercises

What does the term dynamics mean in music?

Write the musical symbol and term for the following directions.

	Symbol	Term
Very soft		
Soft		
Moderately soft		
Moderately loud		
Loud		
Very Loud		
Get louder		
Get softer		
Play one note loud and then get soft		
Play one note very loud		

Lesson 20: Tempo Markings

Another part of the music that the musician needs know is the tempo, or the speed of the music. Some tempos markings are very specific, usually measured by beats per minute. Beats per minute (or BPM) is an exact marking, meaning how many beats take place within one minute of time. Metronomes are set to give the musician the beats per minute. In the music, the type of note that gets the beat followed by an equal sign and then the number of beats in one minute.

♩ = 120

This means that the quarter note gets the beat and there are 120 beats in every minute. The metronome should be set to the number 120.

𝅗𝅥 = 90

This means that the half note gets the beat and there are 90 beats in every minute. The metronome should be set to the number 90.

There are more relative musical terms for tempo. These terms are more general and tell the musician more of an overall speed, rather than a very specific one. Below are some of the most commonly used musical terms to describe tempo. These terms are usually written out in words, as there are no symbols for them.

Largo- very slow

Adagio- slow

Moderato- moderate

Allegro- fast

Presto- very fast

Accelerando- to accelerate, or get faster. Can be abbreviated as "*accel.*"

Ritardando- to ritard, or get slower. Can be abbreviated as "*rit.*"

Tempo Markings Exercises

What does the music term "tempo" mean?

Write the correct way to notate that there would be 140 beats per minute in 4/4 time.

Write the correct way to notate that there would be 75 beats per minute in 3/4 time.

Write the correct way to notate that there would be 58 beats per minute in 6/8 time.

What does the term "Largo" mean?

What is the musical term for "fast?"

In the space below, write the following terms in order from slowest to fastest: Largo, Presto, Allegro, Moderato, Adagio

What does the term accelerando mean?

What does the term ritardando mean?

Write the correct abbreviation for accelerando.

Write the correct abbreviation for ritardando.

Lesson 21: Articulation Markings & Additional Symbols

Articulation is the specific way that notes are played. The following musical symbols are used with specific notes in the music. Unlike accidentals that carry through the measure, these markings only affect the one note:

Symbol	Name	What it does
	Accent	The mark puts an emphasis on one note; the musician plays the affected note louder than others
	Legato/Tenuto	A line above or below the note head; the musician plays the affected note full value, almost connecting notes together.
	Staccato	A dot above or below the note head; the musician plays the affected note short
	Fermata	This symbol is placed above or below the note head; the musician holds the affected note until a cutoff is given from a conductor or bandleader.
	Caesura	Nicknamed "railroad tracks," the musician stops immediately at the symbol. In the example, stopping after the 2nd note without going to the next measure.
	8va	Shown with brackets to show the affected notes. Play one octave higher than written. The symbol is used to make the music easier to read and in the normal reading range.
	8vb	Shown with brackets to show the affected notes. Play one octave lower than written. The symbol is used to make the music easier to read and in the normal reading range.
	Double flat/ Double sharp	Double flat looks like two lower case B's Double sharp looks like an X. Both are twice the amount of regular accidentals, meaning a full step in each direction instead of just one half step.
	Slur	Two different note names tied together; played connected and without a breath in between.

There are some musical symbols that will help with the overall form of the music. While some songs go exactly from the beginning to the end, many songs repeat sections within the music or go back to the beginning or to another specific place and repeat earlier sections. Sometimes after a section is repeated, the musician goes to an ending section of the music, called a Coda.

Repeat Sign
Play the previous measure one additional time. In this example, the musician would play the first measure two times.

Multi-measure Repeat
Play the previous measure the number of times as the number above the repeat sign indicates. In this example the musician would play the first measure 4 times (original measure, then repeat it three more times for a total of 4 times).

Two-bar Repeat
Play the two measures before the repeat sign again. In this example, the musician would play measure 1, measure 2, then measure 1, measure 2.

Multi-measure Rest
Rest for as many measures as the number above indicates. In this example the musician would play the first measure and then rest for 7 measures.

Section Repeat Signs
Play everything inside the signs twice and then go on in the music. In this example, the musician would play measures 1 and 2, then play measures 1 and 2 again.

Ending Barline
Indicates the end of the song. It looks like a regular barline followed by a thicker barline.

Endings

Play through the end of the first ending, then go back to the beginning repeat sign and play through the second ending and then go on. In this example the musician would play the first three measures, then play the first ending and go back to the beginning repeat sign, play through the first three measures again and then skip to the second ending and go on.

D.C. al Fine

D.C. stands for "Da Capo," Italian for "to the head." In music, "the head" is the beginning. Fine is Italian for end. D.C. al Fine means to go back to the beginning and play to the Fine. In this example the musician would play through the 4 measures and then go back to the beginning and play to the Fine at the end of the second measure.

D.S. al Fine   %

D.S. stands for "Del Segno," Italian for "to the sign." D.S. al Fine means to go to the sign and play to the Fine. In this example, the musician would play the 5 measures, then go back to the sign at the beginning of the 3rd measure until the Fine at the end of the 4th measure.

Coda   ⊕

The Coda is the ending section of the song. It is usually a section written outside of the body of the regular music. When reaching the Coda sign in the music, find the Coda sign near the end and skip to that section and play to the end of the song.

⊕ Coda

D.C. al Coda

"Da Capo al Coda" which means "the head, to the Coda." Play to the end of the main section of music and go back to the beginning until the Coda sign and then skip to the Coda section to the end. In this example the musician would play the first 5 measures, go back to the beginning and play to the Coda sign after measure 3, then skip down to the Coda section and play to the end.

D.S. al Coda

"Del Segno al Coda" which means "the sign to the Coda." Play to the end of the main section of music, go back to the sign until the Coda sign and then skip to the Coda to the end. In this example the musician would play the first 5 measures, then go back to the sign, which is at the beginning of the 2nd measure. Then the musician would play the 2nd and 3rd measures and then skip down to the Coda section and play to the end.

Reminder that some music can be played straight through without repeats, endings, or a D.S. or D.C. It is good practice to look all the way through the music and first determine the form of the music before starting to play through it. The overall form of the music with repeats, endings, Coda, etc. is called the "roadmap" of the song.

Articulation Markings & Additional Symbols Exercises

For each music symbol, write the information it gives to the musicians.

Symbol	Name	What it does
	Accent	
	Staccato	
	Fermata	
	Caesura	
	8va	
	Double sharp/ Double Flat	

Write the musical direction given by each musical symbol.

Repeat Sign

Multi-measure Rest

Section Repeat Signs

Ending Barline

Endings

What do the words "Da Capo" mean in English?

What does Fine mean in music?

Describe the difference between "D.C. al Coda" and "D.S. al Coda."

Write the form of the music and what the musician would play below.

D.S. al Coda

Lesson 19-21 Review

Musical symbols give musicians specific instructions on how to correctly perform a piece of music. These symbols give information such as tempo (speed), dynamics (loud or soft), form of the music, and much more.

Dynamics:

pp	Pianissimo- very soft	***p***	Piano- soft
mp	Mezzo piano- moderately soft	***mf***	Mezzo forte- moderately loud
f	Forte- loud	***ff***	Fortissimo- very loud

cresc <   Crescendo, meaning to get louder

decresc >   Decrescendo, meaning to get softer

fp   Fortepiano, play the first note loudly and immediately get soft

sfz   Sforzando, play the note very loud

Tempo:
Some tempo markings are very specific, with a particular number of beats per minute, while other tempo markings are more general.

♩ = 120   This means that the quarter note gets the beat and there are 120 beats in every minute. The metronome should be set to the number 120.

♩ = 90   This means that the half note gets the beat and there are 90 beats in every minute. The metronome should be set to the number 90.

Largo- very slow   Adagio- slow
Moderato- moderate   Allegro- fast
Presto- very fast
Accelerando- to accelerate or get faster. Can be abbreviated as "*accel.*"
Ritardando- to ritard or get slower. Can be abbreviated as "*rit.*"

Symbol	Name/What it does
	Accent Play the affected note louder, with emphasis.
	Legato/Tenuto Play the affected note full value, almost connecting notes together.
	Staccato Play the affected note short
	Fermata Hold the affected note until a cutoff from conductor or bandleader.
	Caesura Stop the music immediately at the symbol.
	8va Play the affected notes one octave higher than written.
	8vb Play the affected notes one octave lower than written.
	Double flat/Double Sharp Play double flatted notes down one whole step. Play double sharped notes up one whole step.
	Slur Two different note names tied together; played connected and without a breath in between.

Repeat Sign
Play the previous measure one
additional time.

Multi-measure Repeat
Play the previous measure the number of times
as the number above the repeat sign indicates.

Two-bar Repeat
Play the two measures before the repeat sign again

Multi-measure Rest
Rest for as many measures
as the number above indicates.

Section Repeat Signs
Play everything inside the signs twice and then
go on in the music.

Ending Barline
Indicates the end of the song.

Endings
Play through the end of the first ending, then go back to the beginning repeat sign and play through the second ending and then go on.

D.C. al Fine
D.C. stands for "Da Capo," Italian for "to the head." In music, "the head" is the beginning. Fine is Italian for end. D.C. al Fine means to go back to the beginning and play to the Fine.

D.S. al Fine ∮
D.S. stands for "Del Segno," Italian for "to the sign." D.S. al Fine means to go to the sign and play to the Fine.

Coda ⊕
The Coda is the ending section of the song.

D.C. al Coda
"Da Capo al Coda" which means "the head, to the Coda." Play to the end of the main section of music and go back to the beginning until the Coda sign and then skip to the Coda section to the end.

D.S. al Coda
"Del Segno al Coda" which means "the sign to the Coda." Play to the end of the main section of music, go back to the sign until the Coda sign and then skip to the Coda to the end.

Lesson 19-21 Test

Write the name and the musical direction for each dynamic marking.

p

mf

ff

cresc   <

Write the proper tempo marking for exactly 120 beat per minute in 4/4 time.

Write in the definitions of the following tempo terms:

Adagio-

Presto-

Ritardando-

For each musical symbol, write the name and the musical direction:

Symbol	Name	Direction

Write in the musical direction for each musical symbol:

1)

2)

3)

4)

Write out the correct "road map" for each music form:

D.C. al Fine

Fine   D.C. al Fine

D.S. al Coda

𝄋   ⊕   D.S. al Coda

⊕ Coda

Lesson 22: Triplets

There is one additional rhythm that we must learn, which is called a triplet. The "tri-" prefix means 3, just like there are three wheels on a tricycle or three sides to a triangle. In music, a triplet has three notes in the space where there is normally two of the same kind of note. We will start with the eighth note triplet. When using regular eighth notes, there are two eighth notes in a beat. With eighth note triplets, there are three notes in a beat.

We have learned to count eighth and sixteenth notes with the & sign as well as "e" and "a." For triplets we must have a different way to count since there are three notes to a beat instead of two or four. The first note is on the beat and uses the count, the second note is called the "trip" and the third note is the "let." See the measure below as we count four beats of triplets.

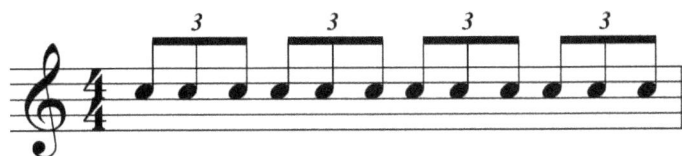

1 trip let 2 trip let 3 trip let 4 trip let

When we shift to quarter note triplets, there are usually two notes within two beats (one beat for each note). But with quarter note triplets, there are three notes within two beats. We count them the same with the beat number, then "trip" and then "let," but we must remember that the full quarter note triplet takes up two beats, the second quarter note triplet starts on count 3. The first example shows the counting, the second example adds in quarter notes on the bottom to show the triplets in relation to the quarter note triplets.

1 trip let   3 trip let

1 trip let   3 trip let

Below are some examples of counting with quarter note and eighth note triplets.

1 - 2   3 trip let   1   2 trip   let 3 trip let 4   1 trip let 3   4 &   1   2 trip let 4

1 2 & 3 4 trip let   1 e & a 2 3 trip let 4   1 trip let 2 trip let 3 4 &   1 trip let 2 trip let 3 trip let 4

Triplets Exercises

Write in the counts for the following examples with triplets. Be sure to check the time signature before starting each line. After writing in the counts, try to count and clap each line.

Lesson 23: Simple & Compound Time

There are two categories of time signatures: simple time and compound time. Simple time is a time signature where every beat is a strong beat. Some examples of simple time are 2/4, 3/4, and 4/4 time. Compound time is a time signature where some beats are strong beats and some beats are weak. Some examples of compound time are 6/8, 12/8, and 7/8. In most even compound times (6/8 or 12/8), the strong beats are evenly and equally spaced. But in most odd compound times (5/8, 7/8, etc.) the strong beats cannot be evenly spaced. The strong beats are a combination of quarter notes and dotted quarter notes. Those time signatures are commonly referred to as "odd time."

In the example of 6/8, there are typically two strong beats, 1 and 4, with 2, 3 and 5, 6 as the weak beats. This creates strong beats of dotted quarter notes, which also makes the eighth notes feel like triplets.

Which sounds like:

Examples of Simple Time, where every beat is a strong beat:

Example of Compound Time, where there is a series of strong and weak beats. In this example of 12/8 there are 4 strong, evenly spaced beats:

Compound time with irregular intervals of strong beats is called "odd time." In many odd time signatures there is more than one feel possible. Underneath the count is an alternate way to count with just eighth notes within strong beats (1-2, 1-2, 1-2-3, etc.)

Simple & Compound Time Exercises

Give two examples of simple time signatures:

Give two examples of compound time signatures:

For each example, write whether it is simple time or compound time. Bonus, put a star next to the "odd time" example:

Lesson 22-23 Review

Triplets are where three notes are in place of where two notes usually fit. For example, eighth note triplets fit in the same space as where two regular eighth notes fit, which is one beat. Three eighth note triplets fit inside one beat. In counting triplets, we start with the beat number, the 2nd note of the triplet is counted "trip," and the 3rd note is counted "let."

1 trip let 2 trip let 3 trip let 4 trip let

When it comes to quarter note triplets, the triplet fits in the space of two normal quarter notes, which is two beats. That means that a quarter note triplet is the same as 2 full beats.

1   trip let   3   trip let

Time signatures can be broken down into two categories: simple time and compound time. Simple time means that each beat is a strong beat. Some common simple time signatures are 2/4 , 3/4, and 4/4 time. Compound time means that some beats are strong and some beats are weak. Some examples of compound time are 6/8, 7/8, and 12/8 time. Compound time can have regular intervals of strong and weak beats, or they can have irregular intervals, which is called "odd time."

Simple time, where every beat is a strong beat and all beats are distributed evenly:

Compound time, where all strong beats are distributed evenly:

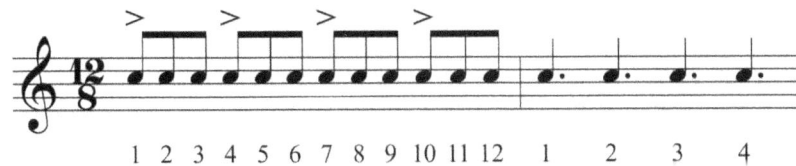

1 2 3 4 5 6 7 8 9 10 11 12   1   2   3   4

"Odd time," which is compound time with irregular sets of strong beats. Notice the strong beats shown in the second measure, which is a quarter note, a quarter note, and a dotted quarter note:

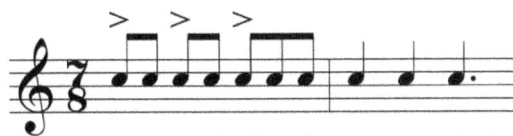

1 2 3 4 5 6 7   1-2 3-4 5-6-7
1 2 1 2 1 2 3   1-2 1-2 1-2-3

Lesson 22-23 Test

Write in the counts for the following lines with triplets. Be sure to check the time signature before starting.

Write for each measure whether it is an example of simple time or compound time.

You've now finished the book! At this point you should have a solid understanding of the basics of reading sheet music, from note reading and rhythmic counting to major and natural minor scales to basic musical terms and symbols. It is important to remember that this book is just the beginning, like a peek into the world of reading and performing music. As started in the beginning of the book, it would be impossible to put everything about music into one book.

What comes next? In terms of music theory, the next step would be learning chords and then on to harmonic analysis. These music theory courses alone can take years, so be patient. Music is a lifelong learning endeavor. As we learned major and natural minor scales, there are 2 more minor scales (harmonic and melodic) as well as the different modes and their respective scales. And there are still many, many more musical terms to learn. And once we learn the basics, we need to develop the ear to bring our listening and comprehension up to what we have learned.

It is important when learning music theory to continue to apply it when studying your main or secondary instrument. Music theory and music performance are not mutually exclusive ideas, they support one another for great learning experiences. The same is true whenever developing a musical ear; the aural skills, the music theory, and the instrumental/vocal performance and study should all go together for a richer and deeper understanding of being a musician. For example, in the next stage when learning chords and harmonic analysis, it is good to also be able to sing the chord outlines and chord progressions, just as it is good to pay attention to it during your instrument/voice studies. Music, as in most things, is not about separate smaller topics, they are all connected together and the sooner we understand that, the sooner we will change the way we study music.

Certificate of Completion

THIS ACKNOWLEDGES THAT

HAS SUCCESSFULLY COMPLETED
FUNDAMENTALS OF READING MUSIC

ADAM BROWN, AUTHOR

TEACHER NAME

About the Author

Adam Brown is a music educator originally from Cincinnati, Ohio. He received both music performance and academic scholarships to attend the prestigious University of North Texas in Denton, Texas, where he earned his Bachelor in Music Education degree (Cum Laude). While at the University of North Texas, Brown studied with Mark Ford, Christopher Deane, Paul Rennick, Ed Smith, and Eugene Corporon. As a student, Brown performed in many ensembles including the renowned UNT Indoor Drumline, winning the Percussive Arts Society Collegiate Championship. During his time at UNT, Brown performed as a part of concerts and clinics throughout the region as well as at the Percussive Arts Society International Convention. Brown won a Texas Percussive Arts Society Scholarship and in 2002, he was one of 25 percussionists worldwide selected to receive an Avedis Zildjian Cymbal Company International Scholarship.

Upon graduating, Brown returned to the Cincinnati area where he taught high school music. He taught percussion, band, marching band, drumline, percussion ensemble, jazz band, guitar, and choir. During his years as a director, the band program performed in concerts and festivals throughout the United States, including the Winter Guard International World Finals, Bands of America Grand Nationals, Ohio Music Education Association State Convention, Bands of America National Concert Band Festival, and the Midwest Clinic. Brown was responsible for creating original curricula for several of the programs at the high school level.

He went on to earn a Master of Science in Education degree (Summa Cum Laude), specializing in the area of Curriculum, Instruction, and Assessment. Through his studies, Brown further expanded his knowledge of building curriculum to meet the needs of students.

After leaving the world of public education, Brown began working for Royal Caribbean International in the role of drummer and Musical Director. Brown worked on several ships in their fleet, performing in nearly seventy countries on five continents. He worked with musicians from around the world and was a part of several new show installs and take-outs.

While working onboard cruise ships, Brown met his wife, Anna Fegi, who was working as a featured singer. Anna has also had a lifelong career in music, working in the recording industry as well as on television and on the stage. They continue to travel and perform throughout the world with Anna's headliner show where Adam is her drummer and Musical Director.

When not performing around the world together, Adam and Anna live in Cebu, Philippines where they are owners of the performing arts school, Brown Academy of Music. They have a passion for sharing their knowledge and love of music to a new generation of music students. Brown is also an artist/endorser for Innovate Percussion sticks and mallets.

www.ingramcontent.com/pod-product-compliance
Lightning Source LLC
LaVergne TN
LVHW061248060426
835508LV00018B/1549